SECOND EDITION

Differentiated Instructional Strategies

for Reading
in the Content Areas

SECOND EDITION

Differentiated Instructional Strategies

for Reading
in the Content Areas

Carolyn Chapman · Rita King

CORWIN
A SAGE Company

For information:

Corwin
A SAGE Company
2455 Teller Road
Thousand Oaks, CA 91320
(800) 233-9936
Fax: (800) 417-2466
www.corwinpress.com

SAGE India Pvt. Ltd.
B 1/I 1 Mohan Cooperative
    Industrial Area
Mathura Road, New Delhi 110 044
India

SAGE Ltd.
1 Oliver's Yard
55 City Road
London EC1Y 1SP
United Kingdom

SAGE Asia-Pacific Pte. Ltd.
33 Pekin Street #02-01
Far East Square
Singapore 048763

Printed in the United States of America.

Library of Congress Cataloging-in-Publication Data

Chapman, Carolyn, 1945-
Differentiated instructional strategies for reading in the content areas/Carolyn Chapman, Rita King. — 2nd ed.
        p. cm.
Includes bibliographical references and index.
ISBN 978-1-4129-7229-1 (cloth)
ISBN 978-1-4129-7230-7 (pbk.)
    1. Content area reading. 2. Language arts—Correlation with content subjects.
3. Individualized instruction. I. King, Rita. II. Title.

LB1050.455.C52 2009
372.41′6—dc22   2009006367

This book is printed on acid-free paper.

09   10   11   12   13   10   9   8   7   6   5   4   3   2   1

Acquisitions Editor:	Cathy Hernandez
Editorial Assistant:	Sarah Bartlett
Production Editor:	Libby Larson
Copy Editor:	Paula L. Fleming
Typesetter:	C&M Digitals (P) Ltd.
Proofreader:	Caryne Brown
Indexer:	Sheila Bodell
Cover and Graphic Designer:	Rose Storey

Contents

Acknowledgments ix

About the Authors xi

Chapter 1: Introduction 1

Infusing Reading Into the Content Areas 1
Sailing Into Differentiated Reading Instruction 1
The Goals of This Book 2
Effective Practices and Related Research 5
Differentiation 7
The Reading Journey 10
Summary 12

Chapter 2: Creating a Climate to Motivate Readers:
Learn to Read With Me 13

Designing the Physical Environment 14
Designing the Affective Environment 16
A Community of Readers 26

Chapter 3: Knowing and Assessing the Reader 27

Developmental Readiness for Reading 28
Meet Your Reading Characters 29
Developing the Eager, Fluent Reader 40
The Keys to Reading Success 42
Five Views of the Reader 42
Assessing and Diagnosing the Reader 49
The Grading Dilemma 58
Summary 59

Chapter 4: Differentiated Models and Strategies of Reading 61

Adjustable Assignment Model 61
Curriculum-Compacting Model 62
Centers and Stations Model 63

Project-Based Models   63

Problem-Solving Model   64

Independent Choice Reading Model   65

Guided Reading Model   65

Language Experience Model   67

Shared Reading Model   70

Read-Aloud Model   70

Four-Block Model   71

From Models to Implementation   72

Summary   80

Chapter 5: Vocabulary   **81**

Identifying and Selecting Vocabulary Words   81

Preassessing Vocabulary Words   82

Learning New Words   84

Twenty-five Ways to Teach Vocabulary   86

Vocabulary Visuals   98

Cues to Context Clues   100

Subject Terminology   101

Overcoming Miscues   102

Master Multiple Meanings   105

Student Mastery of Vocabulary   106

Summary   107

Chapter 6: The Art of Decoding   **109**

Phonics Instruction   109

The Phonics Dozen (The Fonix Duzen!)   110

Structural Analysis   118

Summary   124

Chapter 7: Comprehension and Flexible Grouping   **125**

Why Differentiate Comprehension Strategies?   125

Barriers to Comprehension   126

Levels of Comprehension   127

Steps to Reading a Passage   128

Before Reading: The Passage Preview   129

During Reading: The Passage View   136

Flexible Grouping Designs for Reading Texts (TAPS)   141

After Reading: The Passage Review   147

Assessing Comprehension   160

The Teacher's Role in Comprehension Instruction   164

Summary   166

Chapter 8: Planning   **167**

A Schoolwide Planning Tool: Threading a Reading Skill
    Through the Content Areas   167
Planning to Use Reading Strategies Effectively   168
Planning for Reading of Informational Text   170
Text Check   173
Designing Reading Instruction for English-Language Learners   177
Planning Parent Conferences: Learners Leading the Way   179
Planning Homework Alternatives   179
Planning for Excellence With the Other Three R's   180
Conclusion   181
Differentiated Instruction Is Like a Sailboat Race   181

Appendix   **183**

Recommended Reading   **191**

References   **193**

Index   **197**

ACKNOWLEDGMENTS

Corwin gratefully acknowledges the contributions of the following reviewers:

Anita Price Davis, Professor Emerita of Education
Converse College
Spartanburg, SC

Coleen Martin, Fifth-Grade Teacher
Wilder Waite Grade School
Peoria, IL

Linda Prichard, PreK–Fifth Grade Instructional Specialist
Rutherford County Schools
Murfreesboro, TN

ABOUT THE AUTHORS

 **Carolyn Chapman** continues her life's goal as an international educational consultant, author, and teacher. She supports educators in their process of change for today's students. She has taught in classrooms from kindergarten to college. Her interactive, hands-on professional development opportunities focus on challenging the mind to ensure success for learners of all ages. She believes all students *do* learn. Why not take control by putting excitement and quality into effective learning? Carolyn walks her walk and talks her talk to make a difference in the journey of learning in today's classrooms.

Carolyn authored *If the Shoe Fits . . . How to Develop Multiple Intelligences in the Classroom.* She has coauthored *Multiple Assessments for Multiple Intelligences, Multiple Intelligences Through Centers and Projects, Differentiated Instructional Strategies for Writing in the Content Areas, Differentiated Instructional Strategies: One Size Doesn't Fit All, Differentiated Instructional Management* and the accompanying Multimedia Kit, *Activities for the Differentiated Classroom,* and *Test Success in the Brain-Compatible Classroom.* Video Journal of Education Inc. features Carolyn Chapman in *Differentiated Instruction.* Carolyn's company, Creative Learning Connection Inc., has also produced a CD, *Carolyn Chapman's Making the Shoe Fit,* and training manuals to accompany each of her books. Each of these publications and her trainings demonstrate Carolyn's desire and determination to make an effective impact for educators and students. She can be contacted through the Creative Learning Connection Web site at www.carolynchapman.com.

 **Rita King** is an international consultant. She conducts training sessions for administrators, teachers, and parents at local, state, and international levels. As principal and director of Middle Tennessee State University's teacher-training program in the laboratory school, she taught methods courses and conducted demonstration lessons. Rita's doctorate degree is in Educational Leadership. Her formal training (EdD, ES, MA, and BS) is directly related to education and teacher training. In addition, the state of Tennessee has recognized Rita as an Exemplary Educator.

Rita's areas of expertise include multiple intelligences, practical applications of brain-based research, differentiated learning, reading and writing strategies, creating effective learning environments, and strategies for test success. Her sessions give educators and parents innovative, engaging activities to develop students as self-directed, independent learners. Participants enjoy Rita's practical, easy-to-use strategies, sense of humor, enthusiasm, and genuine desire to foster the love of learning.

Rita coauthored *Test Success in the Brain-Compatible Classroom; Differentiated Instructional Strategies for Writing in the Content Areas; Differentiated Assessment Strategies: One Tool Doesn't Fit All; Differentiated Instructional Management: Work Smarter, Not Harder;* and *Differentiated Instructional Management* Multimedia Kit. She also coauthored training manuals to accompany each of her books.

Rita can be contacted through King Learning Associates Inc., at www.king learningassociates.com, or by e-mail at kingrs@bellsouth.net.

INFUSING READING INTO THE CONTENT AREAS

Every teacher who wants to be a facilitator of learning should also be a reading teacher, because reading is essential in every subject. All teachers know some students struggle to read their texts, while other students sail through material. The learners' reading difficulties become more apparent as they encounter increasingly complex texts and materials in the content areas as they progress through the grade levels. Students need to receive help to develop the skills and strategies necessary to be comprehending, fluent readers and succeed in school and in life.

SAILING INTO DIFFERENTIATED READING INSTRUCTION

Differentiating instruction for reading is similar to the preparation needed for a sailing adventure. The captain identifies each crew member's specialty and talent so assignments can be made in the individual's areas of expertise to make the journey a success. Likewise, all readers have unique skills and talents, as well as the right to learn all the information they possibly can. For this to occur, learning experiences are personalized and individualized during the reading journey.

Teachers are the captains who set the course for the reader's journey, deciding how each one will travel and what each will learn along the way. Differentiated instruction for smooth sailing toward learning and accomplishment is based on effective preassessments of the learner's knowledge, skills, and abilities. It is student centered and flexible because it intervenes and responds to the changing needs of all readers.

Don't you wish you could wave a magic wand and turn every student in your classroom into a comprehending, fluent reader? At the current time, too many learners struggle to read text assignments. Unfortunately, there is no prepackaged, magic formula for teaching students to read. However, educators have the power to create strategies that work for readers of all ability levels by using differentiated instruction. Remember, it is never too late to move students toward their reading potential.

Too much valuable time is expended blaming former teachers, parents, textbook companies, and curriculum programs for the reader's problems. This time and energy can be used productively by diagnosing the student's reading ability and designing customized, successful reading experiences in daily content lessons.

Too often we hear educators beyond the early childhood grades say, "I have too much to do to teach students to read because I have to teach my standards. They should have learned to read in the early grades." This frustration is easy to understand, but remember, the students were taught the skills. They just were not developmentally ready or did not have the strategies for mastering the information.

We cannot afford to let these students go through another academic year without knowing how to read. Reading instruction is a priority in all classrooms. Use every opportunity to intervene and improve a student's reading ability. Transform a struggling student's self-doubt from "I know I can't read," to "I can read!" The smallest improvement has the potential to create a miraculous change in the learner's reading journey.

THE GOALS OF THIS BOOK

This book is designed to assist educators in meeting the unique learning needs of each reader through differentiated instruction. The goals of this resource are to provide the following:

- Reading activities, strategies, and tips for teaching vocabulary, phonics, and comprehension skills
- Techniques and tips for establishing an effective and intriguing reading environment
- Assessment ideas for diagnosing the reader's problems quickly, with suggested prescriptions for solutions
- Memory strategies for a reader to apply to commit information to long-term memory
- Planning tools, including templates, checklists, and guides, to use in reading across content areas

All of our strategies, activities, and ideas are designed to infuse basic reading skills into the content areas. Adapt these tools in planning to meet the needs of individual readers, and make a difference in each learner's academic and personal endeavors.

This resource is grounded in brain-based research, which provides the rationale for the strategies and approaches used. The research includes effective practices related to establishing the learning environment, understanding the reader's problems, and finding solutions.

Our mission in writing this book is to assist teachers in implementing differentiated reading strategies in daily lessons across the curriculum. We hope the activities challenge, actively engage, and empower each struggling student to become an eager, successful reader.

Problems of the Struggling Reader

In our work in classrooms, we have identified four areas that can be barriers for struggling readers. Here we present these areas of concern with some underlying causes for each one.

Vocabulary: Identifying the Word and Its Meaning

- Lack of exposure
- Poor background knowledge
- No prior experiences
- Limited mental word banks
- Minimal knowledge of context clues
- Unable to use dictionaries and glossaries

Decoding: Unlocking the Pronunciation

- Insufficient understanding of letter-to-word relationships
- No ability to identify letter sounds
- Inadequate knowledge of the rules for syllabication
- Insufficient ability to identify root or base words
- Inadequate recognition of prefixes and suffixes

Comprehension: Unlocking Meaning From the Passage or Text

- Inability to find important facts
- Weak inference skills
- Difficulty processing and retaining information
- Calling words without understanding
- Difficulty in getting the "gist" or summarizing
- Lack of strategies and skills to apply automatically

Motivation: Having the Desire to Read

- Sees no need, purpose, or relevance
- Has no internal desire
- Does not make links and connections to his or her world
- Covers up for inadequacies
- Is bored, insecure, or frustrated
- Possesses physical, mental, or emotional blocks
- Has experienced too many prior failures
- Faces lengthy assignments beyond his or her success level

A teacher's major role is to provide the learner with the knowledge base to acquire the needed vocabulary with the essential decoding and comprehension skills to fuel and sustain the desire to read and learn. Design plans to encourage and guide the learner, using tools and strategies such as those outlined in Figure 1.1 (see page 4), until this desire becomes a personal motivating force. The educator's quest is to set an

Figure 1.1 Tools and Strategies for Infusing Reading Into the Differentiated Classroom

Creating the Climate	Knowing and Assessing the Reader	Differentiated Models and Strategies	Vocabulary	Art of Decoding	Comprehension and Flexible Grouping
Physical Environment • Print-rich • Ready resources • Ideal reading spot Affective Environment • Safe • Motivating • Stimulating • Respectful • Choice • Self-efficacy • Celebrating Community of Readers	Developmental Readiness Meet the Reading Characters • Nonreading Nancy • Word-Calling Wayne • Insecure Inez • Turned-Off Tom • Correcting Carl • Read-Aloud Renee • Silent-Reading Sam • Comprehending Carlos Developing the Eager, Fluent Reader Keys to Reading Success Five Views of the Reader • Learning preferences • Gardner's multiple intelligences • Sternberg's triarchic intelligences • Gregorc's learning styles • McCarthy's 4MAT model Assessing and Diagnosing the Reader • Formal and informal tools • Using assessments effectively The Grading Dilemma	Adjustable Assignment Model Curriculum-Compacting Model Centers and Stations Model Project-Based Models Problem-Solving Model Independent Choice Reading Model Guided Reading Model Language Experience Model Shared Reading Model Read-Aloud Model Four-Block Model From Models to Implementation • Agendas/menus • Learning zones, centers and stations • Cubing • On the flip side • Choice	Identifying and Selecting Vocabulary Words Preassessing Vocabulary Words • Color my world. • Meet and greet! • Mystery word Learning New Words • Vocabulary as vocabulary • Word discovery • Adjustable assignments Twenty-five Ways to Teach Vocabulary Vocabulary Visuals Cues to Context Clues • Identifying context clues • Strategies for context clues Subject Terminology Overcoming Miscues • Miscue analysis • What to do with a miscue Master Multiple Meanings Student Mastery of Vocabulary • Mastered words: Check it out! • Teacher-made vocabulary checklists	Phonics Instruction The Phonics Dozen • Understand that letters are symbols for sounds. • Identify the consonants. • Recognize hard and soft consonants. • Recognize consonant blends. • Use the sounds of consonant digraphs. • Recognize long vowel sounds. • Apply the rules for the finale. • Recognize short vowels. • Know the sounds of phonograms. • Recognize vowel diphthongs. • Recognize the controlling r. • Use the proper sounds of y. Structural Analysis • Root words • Prefixes • Suffixes • Syllables • Accent rules and clues	Why Differentiate Comprehension Strategies? • Background knowledge • Interest levels • Ability • Approaches Barriers Levels • Literal • Inferential • Evaluative Before Reading: The Passage Preview During Reading: The Passage View Flexible Grouping Designs • T: Total group • A: Alone • P: Partner • S: Small groups • Differentiated grouping designs After Reading: The Passage Review Assessing Comprehension • Oral reading check • Comprehension checklist • Comprehension reflection self-check • My comprehending way: "How do I comprehend best?" • Running record Teacher's Role

effective course leading each individual to become a motivated, self-directed, successful reader. In the learning journey, each student needs this internal drive to reach his or her reading potential. Thrust is a must!

EFFECTIVE PRACTICES AND RELATED RESEARCH

This book presents strategies, activities, and techniques for improving the performance of all readers. Varied assessments, diagnostic tools, and strategies are emphasized. The following methods and approaches are grounded in brain-based research and effective practices related to teaching and learning. These approaches are essential to improving reading comprehension and are the foundations of the strategies, activities, and ideas in this resource.

Flexible Grouping

In years past, students were placed in ability groups for reading and remained there throughout the year. In today's classroom, ongoing assessment is used to identify strengths and needs. Students are grouped according to their needs as identified in a data analysis. The groups are fluid and flexible to provide the most effective interventions and instructional scenarios for the standard or skill.

Individual Learning Plan

The first Individual Education Programs (IEPs) were used to design instruction for special education students. Currently, many schools design Individual Learning Plans (ILPs) as tools for differentiation to create a program for students at risk. The data gathered are used to target weaknesses and intervene with a plan designed to strengthen those areas. They may be used to customize and personalize instruction for students in general education programs. The information for the ILP may include test scores, learning styles, intelligences, tutoring schedules, mentors, extracurricular activities, academic interests, study habits, health factors, family structure, honors, hobbies, afterschool activities, and work schedules.

Intervention

An intervention is a new direction provided by the teacher for a learner. A new strategy, activity, or assistance is provided as soon as the reader's need is recognized. This is a continuous process for monitoring learning activities and providing improvement approaches as soon as a need is recognized. The need may be identified in a formal assessment or through informal assessments, including observations. An instructional plan is designed for the reader to overcome the deficiency. Often an intervention consists of a mini lesson, clarified directions, or immediate and direct assistance to keep the reader on the right track.

Data-Driven Decisions

Educators are using assessment data to guide the creation of instructional plans in order to reach and teach each reader. They are analyzing and diagnosing each individual's needs to plan productive reading lessons. Students are becoming more involved in the assessment process with immediate feedback, reflections, and self-regulated learning. Data are used to plan independent assignments, to design groups, and to determine how much time is allotted to a specific standard or skill. Data-driven interventions and adjustable assignments maximize learning.

Inclusion

Inclusion meets the needs of a reader who has an identified disability in a regular classroom. The resource teacher or specialist and the classroom teachers work collaboratively to provide the most effective instruction for the student. They bring together the expertise of specialists, staff members, and administrators to benefit the learner.

The student's Individual Education Plan is created through the special education guidelines, which must be followed in daily lesson plans. The plans address the grade-level standards and content information. Each reading activity should be strategically planned to meet the unique requirements of students with special needs. The individual's strengths, including learning styles and intelligences, are engaged in strategies and activities. The reader is provided a supportive environment where he or she feels accepted and valued by all classmates and adults.

Exploring the Verbal Linguistic Intelligence

Howard Gardner (1983), a Harvard psychologist and educator, identified multiple intelligences. The verbal linguistic intelligence includes reading, writing, listening, speaking, and linking information. These abilities and skills are essential for academic achievement and lifelong success. Within this intelligence, a learner may have strengths and weaknesses. Gardner tells us that an area of weakness can be strengthened. This reinforces our belief that it is never too late for students to learn to read.

Schema Theories

Schema theories state new information is constructed to fit information currently existing in the mind. When a teacher introduces a topic, each student has a different schema, or mental picture, the result of prior knowledge and experiences. The new information must be presented so learners "fit" the new learning into their schemas. The ideas existing in a student's mind organize and create meaning from new experiences. This is why it is important to understand and use students' background knowledge to plan effectively for new learning (Piaget, 1952).

Constructivist Learning

Learners play a major role in constructing new knowledge. Vygotsky's and Piaget's work in the later part of the 20th century emphasizes the value of the individual student's role in the learning process. These are the four major components of Vygotsky's and Piaget's theories (Kauchak & Eggen, 2007):

1. Learners construct their own knowledge.

2. Prior knowledge is the foundation for new learning.

3. Social interaction enriches learning experiences.

4. Authentic learning generates personal meaning.

Memory Lanes

Marilee Sprenger (1999) points out that new information enters the brain through the senses. She identifies at least five pathways to memory. The explanations of each pathway can be adapted to teach readers at all grade levels strategies they can use to remember information:

Semantic: Understanding the meaning and purposes

Episodic: Recalling specific events and happenings

Procedural: Using the steps or sequence

Automatic: Applying mastered information without thinking

Emotional: Associating feelings

As you develop lesson plans for specific activities, identify the memory pathway readers can use to store and retrieve the information and skills.

Strategy Ownership

Strategy construction is the discovery of a procedure to use for processing information. Use intriguing strategies to assist readers in learning, storing, and retrieving information. Select activities to engage the readers in their favorite ways to learn. Select and design each one for the student to use independently as needed.

The learner "owns" a strategy when it is used automatically. When the reader takes ownership of a learning tool, it becomes a personal possession to use for a lifetime.

DIFFERENTIATION

The term *differentiation* is defined as a philosophy that enables teachers to plan strategically to reach the needs of diverse learners in classrooms to achieve targeted standards (Gregory & Chapman, 2007). Differentiation meets learners "where they are" in their ability and offers challenging, appropriate options for them to achieve success.

Differentiation shows respect for each reader's learning differences. Everyone has different experiences and brings varied emotions to each learning situation. Not only does the reader have to possess the desire to learn, the individual has to be ready for the information, understand the learning purpose, and make it fit in his or her unique mind.

Differentiating the Content

Educators need to be familiar with grade level standards and then analyze the data to make content selection decisions. Use formative and summative assessments to match the appropriate content with each learner. It is true there is no limit to what a student can learn. If a learner knows the information, the individual needs to move to more challenging opportunities to explore unknown territory related to the current topic. The repetition of mastered information wastes valuable learning time for the student.

Students no longer need to learn the same information at the same time. If the content is too difficult or above the reader's ability level, it is easy for the learner to become frustrated and turned off to learning. This student often experiences the "I can't" feeling. Strategically plan lessons to fill in holes or gaps in learning. Think of the gaps as the missing pieces the reader needs to understand the grade-level standard. Teach the student using content-related materials and resources at the learner's reading level. Analyze the content-related reading material selected for an individual student using a checklist such as the following:

____ Targets the standard or skill.

____ Supports and enhances the current topic.

____ Serves as reference source.

____ Reflects the student's interest.

____ Presents the information in a different genre or format.

Differentiating With Assessment Tools

Use a variety of formal and informal assessment tools to obtain an accurate diagnosis of the reader's needs. If an informal tool provides the needed data, use it instead of the more time-consuming formal tool. With so many standards to teach, so much subject area to address, and so many diverse needs to meet, data-driven instruction is a necessity.

Use an effective preassessment to identify the reader's weaknesses and strengths related to the standard, concept, or skill. To meet the diverse needs of the learner, conduct a preassessment one to three weeks prior to the teaching of the information (Chapman & King, 2008). This provides time to analyze the results, gather materials, create instructional groups and plan strategically for the unique weaknesses and strengths of readers.

Informal assessment tools are quick and easy. Often they indicate how students feel about the information. For example, a teacher asks students to show "thumbs-up" if they understand the lesson segment, "thumbs-to-the-side" if they grasp some of the information, or "thumbs-down" if they do not understand it. The teacher knows immediately by observing where the students are in their understanding of the current concept.

Sometimes it is necessary to administer a more formal assessment to measure the knowledge base and areas of need. In this case, a pretest can be given before the lesson to target strengths and weak areas in the learning. If the same pretest is given to all students, design it so no one makes a perfect score, but for everyone to be able to answer some questions. Be sure the test addresses the needs of those who have little knowledge of the topic, as well as those who are experts. Use the same assessment as a posttest at the end of the study to measure knowledge growth and learning accomplishments. Use a collection of formative and summative assessments to obtain a complete picture of the reader's progress.

During a performance assessment, the reader completes a task that provides evidence of knowledge and understanding. Assessment allows the student to demonstrate how the information is used. Recognize each reader's likes, dislikes, strengths, and weaknesses.

Choice provides the reader opportunities to select preferred ways to demonstrate learning. Identify the student's understanding by asking the reader to choose from a list of assessment options to demonstrate the learning. Encourage the student to use creative approaches to complete the task. Here are some examples of performance assessments:

Reenactments	Demonstrations	Explanations	Musical creations
Exhibits	Posters	Read alouds	Artwork

Differentiating Instructional Strategies

If I can think it, I can say it.

If I can say it, I can write it.

If I can write it, I can read it.

If I can read it, I can decide if I need it.

If I need it, I can decide where and how I can use it!

—Chapman and King

Use a variety of instructional strategies and select the most appropriate one to accommodate the reader's need. Plan assignments so students are actively engaged in the learning. Strategically design each lesson to provide the learner with opportunities to experience challenges, choices, and success to reach reading goals.

Varied instructional strategies target individual needs, using each reader's unique learning styles, modalities, and intelligences. Expectations are determined by standards and reached through strategies and interventions tailored for the reader.

Students need high-level, interesting reading materials and activities to be challenged. These opportunities build reading success. Everyone has a preferred way to attack a passage, solve a problem, and process and retain information. Plan reading experiences to accommodate these preferences and needs.

Make the reading event an exciting happening in the learning journey. Give the students opportunities to use information they have learned. Allow students to work independently in centers or workstations.

Open the door to reading success! Remember, a barrier to understanding is covering material instead of aiming for in-depth understanding. Give everyone's unique brain a true variety of experiences with differentiated instructional strategies.

THE READING JOURNEY

When sailboats leave the shore, they usually have a destination. Often several vessels depart at the same time on their way to a predetermined place. Each craft takes its own course, because there are many routes to the chosen destination.

Curriculum is planned within units of focus because the brain works by making links and connections. The information to be learned during the journey is established, but the components introduced, taught, and explored in each classroom will vary. The standards, goals, and objectives for a given topic may be the same, but each journey will be unique. This is true from class period to class period, from teacher to teacher, and from year to year. The route of the learning journey depends on many factors, including the student's prior knowledge, experiences, and interests; the content information presented; and the teacher's knowledge and presentation skills.

The Captain and Crew

The captain maps the course to the destination. Throughout the trip, changes to the plan require problem solving and decision making. Each crew member on board is assigned specific jobs or roles. Some individuals are experienced; they may train rookie crew members. Teams work together to complete many tasks. Often crew members need to work independently. The captain remains at the helm and oversees the crew's duties and responsibilities.

The Teacher and Students

Like the captain, the teacher guides the learning journey. Educators need to know the reader, the standards, the assessment tools, and the content information to make classroom decisions and establish goals. Through continuous assessment and application of the data to planning, the learning course is designed. Individual and small-group assignments are often leveled or tiered to accommodate the reader's knowledge base, ability with a specific skill, and interest. The teacher is aware of the way each learner approaches a task, problem, or situation. The plans are adjusted through differentiated instruction and interventions to accommodate the reader's changing needs.

The reader's talents, experiences, interests, and prior knowledge are considered, because the individual is a distinct and unique crew member. Each student is responsible and accountable for learning. The reader is guided to be a thinker, doer, risk taker, problem solver, and inquirer. Everyone works well together in the learning community, applying his or her strengths and talents for success while developing a passion for reading.

Assessing the Crew/Revamping the Curriculum

Individual crew members report to the captain and receive feedback when things are going right or wrong. Often the captain doesn't assess the surroundings accurately or does not listen to or heed the danger signals from the crew. The *Titanic*'s captain thought his ship would never sink. He was experienced but did not pay attention to the warnings or the new, correct information. The use of a different maneuver would have placed the ship on another course and saved the vessel.

The teacher must be aware of warning signs, constantly checking with a variety of formal and informal assessment strategies so a different approach or intervention can be used as indicated. Individual reading needs cannot be ignored.

Data-driven plans are made using assessment before, during, and after learning to intervene and change directions. The teacher, as the captain, is in charge and makes the final life-changing decisions for the reader's success or failure.

Design the curriculum plan to create a fail-safe reading journey. The teacher designs the curriculum plan. Sometimes students do not understand the information. Their needs are usually obvious. When these signals indicate a need for review or reteaching for understanding, the students need a new way to work with the materials. Often students become interested in particular topic areas during the learning journey. Take advantage of these learning opportunities and add experiences to meet students' desire to fulfill their curiosity. Use differentiated instruction to provide a variety of strategies for deeper individual understanding and extended learning opportunities to each reader.

Staying on Course

When the destination at sea is not visible, the captain and crew find ways to keep moving in the right direction. They do not give up. They navigate their way to the predetermined goal. Hazards such as storms, high winds, or wave turbulence hinder the sailing vessel and extend the journey. Rerouting is necessary to avoid obstacles. When stormy seas appear, the captain reduces speed or changes routes. It is often necessary to lower the anchor beneath the surface of the water to decrease the vessel's speed. Or it may be necessary to lower the anchor to the sea floor for temporary repairs or adjustments.

Of course, many sailboats complete their excursion on calm seas without being deterred and have no need to make changes in the original plans. Smooth sailing with a "full speed ahead" signal is the ideal experience.

Chart the course for the reader's learning journey. When readers have difficulty with a concept or skill, direct them to the set goals by using a variety of learning strategies, materials, and resources. It may take longer to reach goals and objectives, but the extra time involved in learning a skill is worth it when the reader knows how to apply it and the skill becomes the foundation for new learning. Some readers reach established goals with very little assistance. Encourage students to set independent learning as their reading goal.

SUMMARY

Educators now have the methods, strategies, and materials to assist students in their individual academic excursions in school and throughout life. No longer can we teach to students in the middle ability range and hope that all learners will receive something from the information. Customize experiences to match the reader's needs. The adage "One size does not fit all" reminds us of the need for a major paradigm shift for optimal learning to take place. Customize learning experiences as needed for the student's differentiated reading journey.

CREATING A CLIMATE TO MOTIVATE READERS

Learn to Read With Me

You see words to read almost everywhere,

In books, TV ads, and on the clothes you wear.

Reading opens new doors to worlds of stuff.

Once you start reading, you can't get enough!

Reading takes you to the deepest part of a great sea,

Or to the most remote planets in our galaxy.

Reading introduces you to intriguing people in faraway places.

You hear their lonely cries or see smiles on their faces.

Reading helps you become the person you want to be,

So learn to read wonderful words in our world with me.

—Chapman and King

THE CLASSROOM ENVIRONMENT HAS A MAJOR IMPACT ON student motivation (Jensen, 2008). The teacher's genuine interest and high expectations for students are key elements in the atmosphere of the reading classroom. The students' attitudes toward reading and learning are influenced by the energy and enthusiasm exhibited by the teacher.

An inviting classroom environment promotes learning and motivates readers. Strategically planned activities provide optimal learning experiences. All efforts of the reader are supported in a nonthreatening, comfortable environment.

The reader-environment fit is determined by the influence of the physical and affective factors in the classroom. The physical aspects include the seating and furniture arrangement, visuals, materials, lighting, and temperature. The affective realm includes the teacher's presence, expectations, and personal interactions and the feelings generated by the surroundings in the learning climate. The teacher intentionally plans and maintains an effective physical and affective climate to create the most direct course for the reader to reach personal learning goals.

DESIGNING THE PHYSICAL ENVIRONMENT

Design a Print-Rich Environment

Design a comfortable, personalized place for the students to read. Colorful, high-interest bulletin boards, posters, charts, mobiles, and displays reflect the information taught. Involve the students in setting the stage for learning so everyone has a sense of ownership and belonging. For example, ask the students to design a pictorial time line around the classroom walls, using facts from a current study or a sequence of events from a novel being read to create a colorful, informative border. The students' pride in the designs becomes evident, and the classroom comes alive with the displayed information.

Provide a print-rich environment by asking students to prepare display materials using relevant content information. Use the walls as a study guide for the current information. Include word walls, research data boards, writing reflections, posters, and mobiles. If you teach multiple classes in the room, designate specific areas for group displays. Create attractive galleries with student work so learning becomes a visible reflection of the objectives and standards. Move these visuals to the hall for review when the unit is completed. Begin the process of creating new displays when the next study begins.

Supply Ready Resources

One of the teacher's greatest challenges is to provide ability-level resources and materials that are interesting and intriguing to the reader. Select materials to match the student's ability and knowledge level. Include related fiction and nonfiction books as supplementary resources. Designate a section of the room for these reading materials. Provide various reading materials, including books, periodicals, reference materials, computer programs, and other resources. Remove outdated materials that are not useful to the class members.

Give students time to brainstorm suggestions for materials to add to the resources. This generates a list of items they are interested in reading. Challenge readers to add to the resource center throughout the year. Encourage students to discover places in public, at school, and at home where they can read to get information. Provide "free choice" time for individuals and small groups to browse and read the selected material. This gives students a sense of ownership and personalizes their learning experiences (see Figure 2.1).

Create an Ideal Reading Spot

Provide cozy and comfortable places for students to read. If possible, provide a variety of seating options and allow students to choose where they want to sit to read.

Create Novel Spaces and Places for Readers

Here are some examples:

stool	rug	towel	tree house	sleeping bag
couch	pillow	hammock	stationary bike	lounge chair
boat	tent	treadmill	beach towel	beach chair
loft	cot	rocking chair	glider swing	storage tub
bench	mat	beanbag chair	carpet square	director's chair

Figure 2.1	Reading: Here, There, Everywhere	
Public	*School*	*Home*
Signs	Charts	Labels
Advertisements	Reports	Brochures
Billboards	Graphs	Headlines
Labels	Directions	Letters
Newspapers	Captions	Bills
Store signs	Maps	E-mail
Street names	Glossaries	Web sites
Movie reviews	Instruction sheets	Comic strips
Books	Rules	Catalogs
Magazines	Manuals	Recipes
Maps	Indexes	Calendars
Banners	Diagrams	Reviews
Scoreboards	Schedules	Notes
Brochures	Posters	Directions
Tags	Diaries	Newspapers
Traffic signs	Books	Magazines
Menus	Signs	Manuals
Schedules	Displays	Menus

Props for the Reading Corner

Use props as gimmicks to hook students on reading. Here are some examples:

pens, pencils	pen light	sticky notes
hats, caps	sunglasses	holiday décor
helmets	reading lamp	tape recorder
earphones	MP3 player	background music
toys	CD player	magnifying glass
lantern	bookmarks	stuffed animals
flashlight	content artifacts	

Display Places and Spaces

Display projects in an area for others to learn the information and appreciate the reader's efforts and creativity. Display places may include these:

classrooms	media centers	cafeteria walls	stages
entrances	exits	boxes	ceiling tiles
hallways	foyers	columns	bathroom walls

Display Designs

dioramas	models	posters	mobiles
galleries	scrapbooks	exhibits	recordings
videos	photographs	character museums	performances
puppet theaters	trifold posters	PowerPoint presentations	

DESIGNING THE AFFECTIVE ENVIRONMENT

Anything that touches or stirs a feeling influences the reader's emotions and ties directly to the ability to learn. Everything in the students' peripheral vision plays a role in their affective domain. Be aware of how the environment and emotional connections affect the reader.

Provide a Safe and Accepting Atmosphere

View Errors as Learning Opportunities

Create a learning atmosphere in which the student views reading errors as opportunities to improve rather than memorable embarrassing events. Provide options for the student to obtain extra assistance whenever needed. Strategically plan a psychologically safe environment so the student feels free to take reading risks with questions and thinking.

Develop a Team Spirit for Learning

Choose a team name for the class. Remind students that everyone in the class is on the team. Emphasize the goal is for everyone to learn as much as possible during the semester or year. Display banners using phrases to promote a reading spirit.

Here are some examples:

- Reading makes me a winner.
- Reading takes you to the top.
- Reading trains my brain.

Provide Teaching Opportunities for Students

Give students opportunities to teach each other about the information learned. Organize teaching experiences with individuals or peer groups. Arrange a time for a student to read with other students in other classrooms and grade levels. If time permits, encourage the reader to create a game or activity to accompany the lesson. This gives the student a special avenue to organize, process, and adapt the information read. This time for teaching and reading opportunities is worthwhile because it involves the student in optimal learning experiences. Consider this example of the impact one teaching experience had on a young student's life.

The mother of a fourth-grade student asked a summer school principal to help her daughter, Alex, with reading. The mother said Alex refused to read for pleasure. She had a negative attitude associated with all reading activities.

The principal held brief reading sessions with Alex. They read easy books together. One day, Alex read a Dr. Seuss book by herself. The principal suggested Alex read the book to a kindergarten class and encouraged her to create an activity to use with the book.

After Alex read to the children, she hurried back to the principal's office and said, "Someday I want to be a reading teacher!"

Today Alex is a college graduate. She started reading with enthusiasm the day she read her book and used the activity she had created with the kindergarten children. Alex's mother reports she is an honor student who has been an avid reader since that special day when she discovered the joy of reading to the kindergarten children.

Empathy

Emotions create memorable experiences in learning situations. Design reading activities that stir emotions to create personal connections. For instance, place students "in the author's or character's shoes" so their feelings become an anchor for instruction. Use journaling, character sketches, and reflective questioning activities to record the heights and depths of emotions.

Bibliotherapy heals students' emotional injuries that may be obstacles to learning. When a student is dealing with divorce, family separation, marriage, or new siblings, introduce the learner to books or materials related to the event. The reader develops understanding, empathy, and coping alternatives by reading about other people who deal appropriately with the same experiences.

Rapport

A teacher has a tremendous impact on a student's motivation and desire to read. Learners know when the teacher genuinely cares. This intuitive feeling makes students know they are liked and respected. Students will work hard to please the teacher if they feel acceptance and rapport.

Rapport with the student develops through sharing personal stories, experiences, and common interests. A teacher's excitement in reading about new ideas and facts is contagious. Be a positive role model. Create excitement for learning with observable passion.

Here are suggestions for creating teacher-student rapport:

- Greet students with a smile.
- Take pictures of the class and display them.
- Write specific "praise" notes to students.
- Praise students in front of their classmates and adults.
- Give students a "pat on the back" or a high-five for success as they enter and leave each day.

- Use energizing cheers.
- Plan a picnic, swimming party, or special event for learning celebrations.
- Use humor.
- Praise! Praise! Praise!

Motivation

Motivation is an internal process that guides behavior over time. Intrinsically motivated students tend to enjoy school more and are better readers (Sheldon, Elliot, Kim, & Kasser, 2001). Being motivated keeps readers interested and directs their thinking. Teachers need to find each learner's key to internal motivation. Turned-off students do not learn. The teacher's role in motivating the reader includes the following:

1. *Challenge and stimulate the reader's mind.* Make the reading event interesting and memorable. Build on prior accomplishments and successes. Too many experiences in school are boring sessions that turn students off to reading. Students need more challenging, reading opportunities that are intriguing and exciting.

2. *Set up an effective working environment with established rules.* Be consistent and persistent. Take time to explain the rules so they understand "the way we do things around here."

3. *Recognize and reinforce student's successful accomplishments.* Offer helpful, corrective feedback. Ask thought-provoking questions to develop problem solvers and thinkers. Use specific praise for appropriate behaviors and right answers.

4. *Be dynamic! Think outside the box!* Dare to be different so students never know what stimulating or wacky strategies, activities, or events they will be involved in next.

5. *Adjust assignments to be appropriate for the readers' needs.* Students learn what they want to learn. Accept their unique qualities and strengths. Plan for the diverse needs of readers so they will be able to master the strategies and skills needed to learn, apply, and succeed. Use a variety of approaches. If the task is too easy, the student may not be motivated. There is a high probability of success when the learning becomes a challenge and the reader is motivated to meet it.

6. *Learn about the students' interests and needs* so you truly know how to plan for individual needs. Teach at their optimal learning level.

7. *Encourage interaction* among students by using team learning for activities such as brainstorming, partner reading and writing, cooperative groups, and role-playing.

8. *Provide choices* so students can make decisions about their learning; for example, what they read, where they read, or with whom they read. Accept students' input as to how they can accomplish reading tasks. Invite student involvement. Choice increases student curiosity and reading achievement (Guthrie, Wigfield, & Von Secker, 2000).

9. *Create an internal desire to read.* Remember, attitude is altitude! Encourage each individual to turn "I cannot do this!" to "I can do this!" When readers reach their goals, their accomplishments become personal awards. Praise and reward effort and improvement.

10. *Be positive and show your passion.* Show that you genuinely care. Build a positive relationship with students. Students know when you are sincere and believe they can read and learn.

11. *Create self-directed learners.* Effective teachers help students see the relevance of what they are learning (Assor, Kaplan, & Roth, 2002). Link new learning to their personal experiences. If students feel the information is meaningful and that they genuinely need to know it, they will read it.

12. *Realize that you make a difference.* Every student needs to be motivated to succeed. Demonstrate your belief in each student. Be the change agent in a reader's life.

The differentiated reading classroom shows respect for learner differences. Students bring different experiences and emotions to learning situations. Readers have to be ready for the information, understand the learning purpose, and see where it fits in their unique minds.

Students have a wide range of reading abilities. Each individual has unique physical, emotional, social, and academic needs. Many students have reading skills far below the grade level of the text and supplementary materials. Struggling readers may bring diverse cultural and economic backgrounds to the classroom. Teachers are expected to meet the needs of these struggling, reluctant readers, as well as those of the enthusiastic, talented readers.

Often a learner's negative attitudes toward reading are the result of experiences with past failures. In the early grades, a student uses easy, reader-friendly, fact-filled texts and fictional materials. Adult assistance and guidance are available. As the reader moves through the grades, however, books and factual materials become more complex and difficult. The student is expected to complete learning tasks independently. A reluctant reader may not succeed because of constant struggles with comprehension of texts and supplementary grade-level materials. A capable reader may not reach reading potential because of continued struggles with boring, unchallenging material. To meet the needs of all learners, present stimulating and engaging lessons on all the readers' ability and interest levels.

How do teachers find time to teach basic reading skills and strategies to these diverse learners when they are required to teach the subject standards, skills, and objectives effectively? They infuse reading strategies in novel and engaging ways with topic-related information. The learner's focus remains on the content information. This challenges and motivates students to *want* to read.

William Glasser's choice theory of motivation (Glasser, 1990, 1998) cites five important student needs for learning motivation. Carol Ann Tomlinson and colleagues' *Parallel Curriculum* (2002) also names five motivating needs to incorporate when inviting students to learn. Figure 2.2 on page 20 adapts the views of Glasser and Tomlinson et al. to the reading classroom.

Figure 2.2		Needs for Reading Motivation
Glasser's Needs	Tomlinson's Needs	The Effective Classroom Culture Provides the Reader With . . .
To survive and reproduce	Affirmation	Basic needs Acceptance A meaningful place in the learning culture Membership in a group
To belong and be loved	Contribution	Experiences that make a difference Opportunities to make contributions to the class A nurturing environment Acceptance A risk-free environment Freedom for expression
To have freedom	Purpose	Exploration and discovery Opportunities with decision making and problem solving Self-efficacy
To have power	Power	Opportunities to make decisions Choices Active learning Understanding of purpose, directions, and goals Empowerment
To have fun	Satisfaction	Challenges to stimulate the mind Activities of interest Choices Work in comfort zones Active learning Humor and fun

Flow

The state of flow occurs when a learner is doing something that occupies and stimulates the mind (Csikszentmihalyi, 1990). For instance, when an individual reads something of high interest, the reader may become totally focused on the information and unaware of the surroundings. During this time, the reader is in a state of flow.

Students often go through an entire school day and never experience the state of flow. Teachers can identify a learner's areas of strong interest through observation, inventories, surveys, and conversations. Use this information in lesson plans to capture the reader's attention and interest.

Recent studies of magnetic resonance images (MRIs) and the workings of the brain (Sousa, 2005) show that after a person is engaged in the state of flow, then during the next activity, no matter how difficult, the individual's performance is better and the ability to concentrate is heightened.

Attention, Challenge, Excitement, and Humor

Students spend too many hours reading boring text, completing routine worksheets, or working with meaningless activities. Texts, worksheets, and assignments are more effective when the teacher makes the content come alive, generates curiosity, and creates excitement in relation to the tasks.

Students deserve teachers who care about them and believe they can read. They deserve teachers who can immerse them in reading material and challenging activities that support and enrich their goals and dreams. Make their learning interesting, challenging, and exciting by varying your strategies. Humor creates a personal connection with the information and with the teacher. A good laugh relaxes the brain and prepares it for more information.

Grab the Reader's Attention

Select materials to generate curiosity and interest. Use challenging, fun resources and activities that stimulate the mind and set a positive classroom tone.

Here are some examples:

- Jokes, songs, sayings, riddles, cheers, mind twisters, or poems
- Biographies of movie stars, popular singers, music groups, or role models
- Intriguing, challenging questions that lead the student to think and want to read for more information
- Game show formats

Use Anticipation Carrots

Anticipation carrots lead the student to look forward to upcoming learning encounters. Announce high-interest resources, experiences, or activities before formally presenting them. These phrases stir curiosity and focus the mind on future learning:

- Read this to discover . . .
- Read this and then you will share what you learned with a classmate.
- You are going to like this.
- When you read this, you are going to find out . . .
- At the end of the unit, we will . . .
- Guess what we will do with this information tomorrow!
- Think of ways we can have fun using the information we learned today.

Interweave Interests

Many students are fans of sports heroes, actors and actresses, rock stars, and well-known book characters. Know the students' heroes and special interests so they can be incorporated as valuable tools to reach the readers in instructional activities. Learn about individual interests and desires through conversations, conferences, surveys, inventories, and journals. Know each learner's interests or hobbies so well that it is easy to carry on a casual conversation with the student.

Challenge the Mind

Create opportunities for students to work with higher-order thinking skills and mind-challenging activities as they learn new information. Establish an environment where the students yearn to participate and their desire to learn is cultivated daily.

Respect

Choose words and terms to set a positive tone in the classroom. When a student is treated in a kind and respectful way, the student learns to reciprocate. Give specific praise of observable behaviors. Always avoid negative words and phrases such as "You can't . . . ," "If you don't . . . ," and "That's wrong!"

Use words and phrases that reflect respect for the student, such as the following:

Please.	Be careful when . . .
Pardon me.	You'll like this better.
Let me help you . . .	Are you comfortable?
I like the way you . . .	You did that well because you . . .

Successful experiences and praise increase students' motivation or desire to read. The teacher's enthusiasm for reading and creating the learning environment has a major impact on the readers' interest. Positive interactions while reading with a parent, partner, or small group enhance motivation.

Choice

Intrinsic motivation increases when students are provided with choices in their learning activities (Stipek, 1996). According to Eric Jensen (2008), providing choices is the key to motivation. Jensen emphasizes the role of the teacher in finding ways to reach the unmotivated learner. The student needs opportunities to select reading materials, research methods, activities, presentation strategies, reporting formats, and evaluation tools.

Choice is a motivational tool. Use it to build on the student's interests. It is an effective way to develop confidence, foster independence, and create a sense of responsibility during reading experiences.

Choice Boards

Strategically design a choice board containing mind-challenging activities (see Figure 2.3). This is an effective way to give students voices in their reading. Students

Figure 2.3 Choice Board		
Design a game based on the subject's facts and trivia.	Write a song that includes the important information.	Create raps, rhymes, or riddles using the vocabulary terms.
Write and illustrate a mini book based on the facts.	Write a front-page news article that includes important facts and details of an event.	Dramatize the procedures, stages, steps, or events in a passage.

enjoy selecting the activities to show what they know, to learn more about the topic, or to apply information in new and different ways. Choice boards provide innovative ways for students to show what they have learned from a text passage, a specific reading selection, a unit, or a subject.

The Teacher's Role in Providing Choices

1. Create choice activities based on the reader's needs, ability, and interests.

2. Limit the number of choices if the reader lacks experiences in making choices. Here are some choice board examples:
    - A four square outline to design 4 choices
    - A tic-tac-toe grid to design 9 choices
    - A bingo board to design 25 choices
    - The shape of an object from a unit or story
    - A holiday or seasonal board

3. Provide the reader with opportunities to design activities.

Self-Efficacy

Self-efficacy is an individual's belief in his or her own ability. Teachers with strong self-efficacy know they use effective classroom management, make learning exciting for students, incorporate the most appropriate resources, and engage parents in positive ways (Bandura, 1997). Self-efficacy is an internal motivator for students, too. Learners who believe they cannot read probably will not be as successful as students who believe they are competent readers.

The Teacher's Role in Building Self-Efficacy

Teach the reader to use self-praise for reading experiences. Here are some examples:

- I enjoyed reading this passage because . . .
- I learned the facts when I read about the topic.
- I am glad I can understand this.

Provide reading models for the reader to imitate. Here are some examples:

- Listen to recordings of books and poems related to the subject.
- Invite specialists in the subject area to read and share information with the students.
- Give the reader opportunities to read to classmates or students in lower grade levels.
- Set aside a time for the reader to share successful reading experiences.
- Provide peer-to-peer reading opportunities with partners or small groups.
- Plan a time to model reading daily.
- Use celebrating cheers.

Celebrate Reading Achievements

Emphasize the value, self-satisfaction, and joy that come during the reading process. These feelings can be described as personal celebrations.

You can encourage students to read by planning celebrations. Students are eager to read when they are looking forward to these events. Include total class and schoolwide galas to honor readers.

Classroom Reading Celebrations

Try one of these celebrations for each book read:

- Place a marble in a large glass jar.
- Write the name of the book and the author and student's critique on a card to display.
- Add a candle to a cake.
- Add a spot on a leopard.
- Place a button on a bear.
- Place a sticker in a class book.
- Add a page to the class diary of reading reviews.
- Place the name, author, and review on a book shape and hang it on a string for a book clothesline.
- Decorate a door, hallway, side of a cabinet, or bulletin board with reading lists or critiques of completed books.

Schoolwide Reading Celebrations

When a school meets a reading goal, an activity can be planned as a unique or crazy celebration. If a teacher or a member of the school staff performs one of the following actions, the students will experience a day that rewards and celebrates reading while also creating memories that connect exciting experiences with reading.

- Sit on the school roof for a day in a lounge chair with an umbrella, book, and picnic basket of goodies.
- Perform a favorite song during a reading rally.
- Kiss a pig.
- Have an "Eat Up Reading" adventure after school hours or at a set time during the day. This can be a readathon or a shared reading experience with pizza, popcorn, or other snacks donated by local business partners or parent groups.
- Shave the head of a staff member or local celebrity.
- Add a celebration corner in honor of the readers to decorate the school. Post an award certificate nearby that recognizes the success.
- Wear mismatched clothes for a Wacky Wednesday.
- Add a fish tank to the hall or media center.
- Host a storytelling session where students tell their favorite stories or invite a guest storyteller.
- Give a party with cake to celebrate reading.
- Read a special story to a class in an assembly or over the intercom.
- Plan a special visitor surprise; for example, a favorite author, war hero, role model, or cartoon character.
- Set a schoolwide time for no homework.
- Hold a special event happening at school. For example, plan a "rock and read" day, play day, musical field day, or character day.
- Host a VIP (very important person) "Read a Book Day." Invite special visitors to come and read to the classes. Consider parents, relatives, administrators, community leaders, older students, retired citizens, and local heroes as VIP readers.
- Hold a pep rally with cheers and banners for reading.
- Sponsor a "Books on Parade" or "Character Debut," with students and school personnel dressed as characters being studied.
- Design a T-shirt about a favorite book and assign a day to wear it.
- Provide buttons or pencils with reading slogans.
- Swap teachers or classes for read-aloud sessions.
- Have a student or teacher tell about a book or read a selection from a favorite book on the intercom each day or on a special day each week.
- Recognize reading success during morning announcements, in hallway news flashes, or in school newspapers.

A COMMUNITY OF READERS

Readers need to know the important role they play in the learning culture as members of the team or crew. In this environment, they know their diverse strengths and needs are honored. They know corrected errors move them to new learning. The inviting reading climate fosters on-task behavior, innovative thinking, and active learning that challenge the mind. In the differentiated reading classroom, all readers in the community of learners know their uniqueness is accepted and honored.

Teachers Who Become Legends in Learners' Lives

A teacher becomes a legend in students' lives by showing genuine care and concern for the pupils' well-being. A teacher's daily interest in students may change the direction of their lives. Struggling readers require nurturing. Students need to know someone cares and will meet their specific needs. Learners live up to high expectations when they want to please their teacher. When a learner's strengths are emphasized and when a success is praised, those become small steps toward permanent change in the student's education journey.

The differentiated reading classroom is an environment that reflects the teacher's joy of learning information in a subject. The student reader observes the teacher's daily enthusiasm and interest in lessons through the evidence exhibited in presentations, daily routines, body language, and conversation. The student is molded by the teacher's belief in his or her ability and by the teacher's high expectations.

> *By helping students find the pleasure in learning, we can make that learning infinitely more successful.*
>
> —Wolk (2008, p. 8)

Knowing and Assessing the Reader 3

By placing the focus where it needs to be—on the individual student—great teachers of reading effectively differentiate instruction and improve the odds for all students.

—Marie Carbo

Meet the Cast of Reading Characters Introduced in This Chapter

Nonreading Nancy
: Reads very little and lacks comprehension skills.

Word-Calling Wayne
: Reads one or two words at a time with little fluency and lacks comprehension skills.

Insecure Inez
: Capable of reading but is afraid of making mistakes. This student comprehends but does not have the confidence to answer questions.

Turned-Off Tom
: Capable of reading and comprehending but does not like to read. Often displays a bad attitude toward reading assignments.

Correcting Carl
: Blurts out correct and incorrect answers out of turn. Does not know how to wait to be called on to speak and share.

Read-Aloud Renee
: Is an auditory learner who comprehends when reading aloud or when someone else is reading.

Silent-Reading Sam
: Comprehends when reading information silently. He is a fluent oral reader but comprehends best with the words in front of him.

Comprehending Carlos
: Is a fluent, comprehending reader.

Plan strategically to know each student so you can guide each one to his or her full potential as a reader. The term *diversity* often refers to cultural background, learning styles, and socioeconomic status. But consider the many ways readers are diverse:

Gender	Socioeconomic status	Ability
Experiences	Knowledge base	Personality type
Learning styles	Intelligences	Self-concept
Attitude	Physical appearance	Study ethics
Behavior	Learning preferences	Emotions
Values	Goals and dreams	Fears
Interests	Language development	Talents and strengths
Ethnicity	Cultural background	Family support

Begin the quest to know each reader by exploring the students' backgrounds and experiences with language. Strong indicators of skill readiness include writing, speaking, and listening. These skill levels affect the learner's emotions and attitudes toward reading.

How can teachers find time to plan differentiated reading strategies for all students? Time invested in viewing the mission and planning the trip step-by-step pays off on the journey. It is worth the time to plan for differentiated instruction because each student benefits with a customized reading itinerary.

DEVELOPMENTAL READINESS FOR READING

The early developmental stages of learning have a major impact on a student's ability and attitudes toward learning to read. Before a child is born, language is developing from the voices and sounds heard. Before the child enters school, oral language develops through mirroring other individuals. Children exposed to language in print on a regular basis are more prepared for reading. When youngsters enter school, it becomes the responsibility of educators at all grade levels to provide appropriate experiences for developing listening, speaking, reading, and writing skills.

A preschool student who climbs, experiments with musical beats, builds and manipulates objects, role-plays, and communicates is preparing the brain for the reading process. As a child explores, discovers, invents, and plays in the creative world, mental pathways for learning develop. These early active experiences enhance the ability to learn throughout life.

One student may blossom as a reader earlier than another of the same age. However, a student who learns to read later may become a stronger reader because the intervening activities developed small and large motor skills, eye-hand coordination, spatial reasoning, and higher-order thinking skills.

A student may become a comprehending reader in the upper grades when reading problems are overcome. This occurs when the student's problems are diagnosed correctly and the student learns to apply reading strategies automatically. An older struggling reader often deals with low self-concept, lack of confidence, lack of motivation, and weak social relationships. Often, this student is motivated by a caring teacher or role model who intervenes with personalized instruction for the needed reading skills.

MEET YOUR READING CHARACTERS

Most classrooms have students with characteristics similar to the reading characters described in the following section. Plan strategically to identify each learner's reading behaviors that reflect unique characteristics and diverse needs. The student's feelings directly influence his or her emotions and attitudes toward the reading process. The ability to read can progress with the suggested prescriptions and solutions.

Use the outline that follows with the titles and subheadings as an observation tool to explore each reader's needs, to understand the student, and to make assessments. Consider the behavior traits and add other descriptors. As the student's reading problems are identified, use the outline and suggested prescriptions as a guide to finding solutions.

Reading behaviors: Identify the learner's specific, observable behaviors during reading activities.

Feelings of the student: Consider the individual's emotions and reactions to reading experiences.

Diagnoses: Analyze the insights obtained from observations and assessment tools to determine the causes of the reading-related behaviors.

Suggested interventions: Select appropriate solutions to the diagnosed problems using the reader's identified behaviors and feelings. Note that the interventions listed here are just a small selection of possible solutions.

Nonreading Nancy

Nonreading Nancy lacks the skills to become a fluent reader. This student reads below grade level. She struggles with comprehension, phonics, and vocabulary. Feelings of defeat have turned off her desire to read. An older student is more likely to hide the inability to read and comprehend. The nonreader at any age deserves the right to be a comprehending reader.

Observed Reading Behaviors

Reads very little.

Reads a few words on grade level.

Exhibits poor comprehension skills.

Does not like to read.

Struggles with word attack skills.

Has limited language ability.

Feelings of the Student

I feel lost when I read.

I will never learn to read, so I will be in this grade the rest of my life.

I cannot read this assignment.

I am embarrassed to read, so please do not call on me.

This is boring and frustrating.

Diagnosis and Suggested Interventions

Unmotivated

Pass on the joy and love of reading through modeling it.

Provide a variety of high-interest, low-level materials.

Read information aloud or taped as the learner follows the print.

Create a print-rich environment.

"Read to" often.

Has a Limited Reading Vocabulary

Use language experience activities.

Play games with vocabulary words.

Engage in conversations and discussions related to the current study.

Use repetitive rhymes and short stories.

Learn basic sight word lists.

Needs Word Attack Skills

Model each new word attack strategy repetitively.

Teach decoding skills.

Use word families to teach patterns.

Arrange for someone to read to her often.

Give the student opportunities to read her own writing.

Lacks the Skills to Bridge Letters to Words, Words to Sentences, and Sentences to Paragraphs

Reteach, expose, or teach these skills.

Use letter and word manipulatives.

Create opportunities for the student to read personal writing, such as journals.

Use computer programs and other technology resources.

Engage in a variety of listening activities.

Lacks Desire to Read Because of Past Failures

Provide reading choices.

Create an atmosphere of excitement.

Implement intriguing prereading activities.

Select guided strategies for success.

Allow the student to interpret information using pictures and graphics.

Give opportunities to read easy books in areas of interest.

Share stories, books, and poems with repetitive rhythms.

Arrange for the student to read easy books to younger students.

Struggles With the English Language

Read stories in the native language and in English.

Use picture vocabulary cards with the words written in both languages.

Label objects in the learner's first language and in English.

Use actions to demonstrate verbs as they are pronounced.

Provide a vast amount of oral and written communications in both languages.

Word-Calling Wayne

Word-calling Wayne concentrates on one word at a time, examining the letter sounds before attempting the pronunciation. Listeners become impatient. The reader becomes embarrassed. Word calling hampers comprehension.

Observed Reading Behaviors

Reads one or two words at a time.

Lacks oral reading fluency and comprehension.

Does not enjoy reading.

Reacts negatively when asked to read aloud.

Feelings of the Student

I hope no one asks me to read aloud.

I know I cannot read as well as my friends.

I understand more when someone reads to me.

I read it, but I do not know what it says.

I read it, but I do not know the answers to these questions.

I am embarrassed every time I read aloud.

Diagnosis With Suggested Interventions

Sees One Word at a Time; Eyes Do Not Move Quickly Across the Line

Model reading using short, easy, familiar passages. The student's eyes follow the words.

Train the eyes for left-to-right movement.

Move a finger or pointer in a continuous rhythm across the lines of writing.

Move a pen light steadily across the lines while reading.

Teach skimming and scanning skills.

Use choral and echo reading.

Use assisted reading and gradually remove support.

Overuses Phonics

Build word recognition speed using repetition of familiar words, phrases, and sentences.

Use a timer to record and increase reading pace.

Say the unknown word for the reader to maintain fluency.

Model sounding out words in the content areas.

Embed word families in unit lessons.

Model fluent reading.

Use games and timed activities to build recognition of basic sight vocabulary words.

Work on letter-word connection.

Teach unfamiliar words in isolation before reading.

Works for Perfection

Teach the value of using various decoding skills to unlock letter sounds.

Provide opportunities for listening and reading with a model.

Use partner-reading activities.

Make stories and books on tape available.

Consider the reader's insecurity when making assignments and activities.

Lacks Rhythm and Flow While Reading

Listen to recorded books and follow the words.

Read and reread easy books.

Read with a model reader.

Read and reread familiar passages from the text.

Work for perfection on one phrase or sentence before trying another sentence.

Does Not Follow Punctuation Symbols

Teach punctuation meaning and rules.

Emphasize punctuation with an action for each symbol; for example, finger snap = period.

Demonstrate and practice use of each punctuation with color coding. Example: red = period.

Use a sound for each punctuation symbol. Example: making a short whistling sound followed by a "pop" sound made with the lips = exclamation point.

Needs Confidence

Read along with recorded books and stories.

Provide easy reading materials.

Practice reading repetitive phrases and rhymes.

Arrange for the student to listen to stories.

Provide reading through language experience activities.

Plan time for the student to read easy books to younger children.

Has a Limited Reading Vocabulary

Play games with words in daily conversations.

Provide a print-rich environment at school and home.

Encourage classmates and adults to carry on conversations related to the content lessons and experiences.

Use read-along strategies.

Insecure Inez

Insecure Inez does not want to make reading mistakes in the presence of others. Low self-esteem is evident. This student does not have a sense of belonging. An inadequate knowledge base in one subject may be the source of the insecurity This insecurity may not be evident in another subject.

Observed Reading Behaviors

Uncomfortable with reading capabilities.

Afraid of mistakes and failure.

Hesitant to demonstrate ability.

Cowers to avoid being called on.

Feelings of the Student

I don't want to be wrong.

I hope no one laughs at me.

I do not believe I can do this.

I don't want to disappoint my teacher, my parents, or myself.

If I read slowly, I will not make as many mistakes.

I dread all reading assignments.

Diagnosis and Suggested Interventions

Afraid to Read

Build confidence with easy reading materials related to the topic.

Ask questions that are easy to answer.

Find the learner's "best" way to read and comprehend.

Read orally with a trusted classmate.

Feels Peer Pressure

Select learning opportunities for success.

Work with small-group instruction.

Provide partner choice for reading experiences.

Encourage the reader to volunteer for oral reading.

Provide individual instruction.

Permit the learner to work alone.

Shy and Nervous

Allow a longer wait time for responses.

Use choice boards.

Provide opportunities for the student to respond privately to questions.

Give short assignments designed to provide success.

Give the reader opportunities to choose a respected or admired reading partner.

Use one-on-one instructional strategies.

Praise each success.

Experienced Too Many Failures and Negative Feedback

Survey to identify interests, attitudes, and feelings related to reading.

Use the learner's knowledge base to develop instructional plans.

Provide confidence-building opportunities.

Give specific praise and positive reinforcement.

Turn "I can't" attitudes into "I can" feelings.

Has Created Emotional Barriers to Learning

Provide easy, enjoyable reading materials.

Give high-interest, challenging assignments at the reader's level.

Give choices.

Showcase the student's talents.

Brag about the student's strengths and successes.

Provide opportunities for the reader to share knowledge of topics and interests.

Turned-Off Tom

Turned-Off Tom is capable of reading and comprehending but is unchallenged and unmotivated. This student needs strong "buy-in," or interest, in the reading activity or assignment.

Observed Reading Behaviors

Exhibits a negative attitude toward most reading assignments.

Often refuses to complete reading activities and assignments.

Doesn't see a purpose for reading.

Reflects a "don't care" attitude through body language and demeanor.

Feelings of the Student

I do not need to read this.

I don't like to read.

Why would I want to waste my time reading this boring information?

I wish these teachers would "get with it" and find something I want to read.

Diagnosis and Suggested Interventions

Needs Positive Experiences in All Reading Activities and Assignments

Provide a nonthreatening environment with a comfortable spot to read.

Read high-interest selections to model reading.

Assign short passages.

Provide materials and assignments in the reader's interest areas.

Use high-interest, auxiliary texts on the student's reading level.

Conduct conferences to give the student opportunities to verbalize feelings related to reading.

Use immediate, specific, positive feedback.

Needs Choices Around Interests

Provide high-interest books and materials.

Select a wide variety of materials at various reading levels.

Provide choices in reading topics and genres.

Use a survey to match books to the reader's interest areas.

Ask the reader to choose books for the classroom library.

Give students opportunities to make reports, exhibits, and presentations related to the reading assignment.

Needs to See Significance in the Reading Activity

Create effective prereading experiences.

Present each assignment with a meaningful purpose that illustrates the student's need to read the information.

Provide interesting follow-up activities based on the reading passage.

Correcting Carl

Correcting Carl blurts out the pronunciation of a word or an answer for a classmate. Often, this learner is unconscious of disruptive, inappropriate behavior when making comments. When the reading pace is too slow, corrections are volunteered to speed along the reading process. It is easy to squelch enthusiasm, but this student must learn to respond when it is his turn.

Observed Reading Behaviors

Blurts out inappropriately.

Answers out of turn.

Lacks respect for others.

Needs and yearns to be heard.

Thinks best when thinking aloud.

Feelings of the Student

I know this answer. I am so proud of myself.

When I say a word aloud, I understand it.

When I know the answers, everyone needs to hear me.

I need to help my friends.

Diagnosis and Suggested Interventions
Wants to Be Heard

Make the student aware of expectations for listening.

Have a private conference to discuss the rules for taking turns.

Explain the need for other students to have a chance to respond.

Provide opportunities for the student to assist readers through small-group or partner activities.

Eager to Move On, So Answers for Classmates

Establish rules for taking turns.

Teach appropriate listening tools.

Teach respect for classmates and adults.

Establish a private reminder signal between the student and the teacher.

Establish a self-monitoring system.

Has Nervous Energy

Provide prompts and signals as reminders.

Reward correct behavior with specific praise.

Provide challenging opportunities and activities.

Actively engage the student.

Permit the reader to work independently in a center or station.

Read-Aloud Renee

Read-Aloud Renee is an auditory learner. She has to hear the words to comprehend. She is an excellent oral reading volunteer because she reads enthusiastically and comprehends. During silent reading, this student often has difficulty understanding the information.

Observed Reading Behaviors

Comprehends when reading aloud but does not comprehend during silent reading.

Has a strong sight vocabulary.

Volunteers to read orally.

Reads aloud with confidence, enthusiasm, and expression.

Needs oral reading to comprehend.

Feelings of the Student

I like to read to others.

I wish I could read with a partner.

I do not like to read silently.

I wish I had someone to read all of my assignments to me.

Diagnosis and Suggested Interventions

Has Difficulty Reading Silently

Play silent comprehension games.

Use brief passages for silent reading assignments.

Provide a private space for reading chosen by the student, if possible.

Maintains a Strong Reading Vocabulary

Reinforce and add to the student's vocabulary knowledge base.

Provide materials that challenge and provide success.

Involve the reader in oral discussions to enhance comprehension.

Possesses a Reading Passion

Provide opportunities to read aloud for varying purposes.

Use a variety of reading materials on high-interest content at challenging levels.

Read aloud to the student.

Allow the student to read to others in lower grades.

Engage in partner and small-group reading experiences.

Has Mastered Oral Reading Skills

Permit the student to share personal fulfillment and success from reading.

Nurture the talent! Be careful not to take advantage of it.

Provide special reading privileges in read-aloud sessions.

Engage the learner in self-recording activities for listening.

Needs to Lip-Read and Mumble During Silent Reading

Understand the reader's need to lip-read and mumble for comprehension.

Isolate the reader so other students are not disturbed.

Teach the student to lip-read without mumbling.

Allow the student to read into an elbow-shaped pipe. Hold the pipe in the position of a telephone receiver so the student hears herself while reading.

Silent-Reading Sam

Silent-Reading Sam comprehends when reading to himself. When he reads orally or someone reads to him, however, he does not comprehend as well. As an older student, he does not volunteer to read aloud unless he has had time to practice reading the selection. This student is strong academically and an effective reader throughout his lifetime, because most reading is usually completed independently.

Observed Reading Behaviors

Comprehends while reading silently.

Has a strong sight-reading vocabulary.

Uses context clues.

Does not comprehend as well when read to or when he reads aloud.

Enjoys reading and is more productive during silent reading.

Feelings of the Student

I know what the author is saying when I read to myself.

No one can correct my reading and embarrass me, if I read alone.

I can read this book at my own pace in my own way.

I need to read this information to myself.

I do not understand it when you read aloud, unless I can follow the words.

I hope I am not called on to read aloud.

Diagnosis and Suggested Interventions

Strong, Independent Silent Reader

Provide time for this student to read independently.

Provide time for the student to read the assigned passage silently before reading it aloud.

Give opportunities to choose reading materials to read silently.

Provide silent reading time before answering comprehension questions.

Weak in Auditory Skills

Make arrangements for the student to read with a stronger reader.

Allow the student to read along with a tape, CD, or computer program.

Use shared reading activities.

Provide a script for the student to follow during read-aloud activities.

Assign short passages for reading.

Build confidence by asking explicit questions following oral readings.

Views Oral Reading as a Time Waster

Provide partner and small-group read-aloud activities with short segments.

Use specific, positive feedback with praise for oral reading.

Give specific purposes for oral reading experiences.

Comprehending Carlos

Comprehending Carlos understands reading passages during silent and oral reading. This student is a fluent reader who enjoys reading experiences.

Observed Reading Behaviors

Comprehends as an oral or silent reader.

Enjoys reading.

Understands, interprets, and adapts information before, during, and after reading.

Has strong word attack skills and a large sight vocabulary.

Understands the reading process.

Feelings of the Student

I like to read.

I know what the author is telling me.

I do not always understand why others struggle with reading.

I wish I could read what I want to read.

I wish I could answer these questions without waiting on everyone.

Diagnosis and Suggested Interventions

Needs Challenge With High-Interest Materials

Provide reading choices.

Make a wide variety of reading materials available.

Assign readings in various genres.

Provide opportunities to share personal enthusiasm as a fluent reader.

Needs Higher-Order Thinking Activities

Assign reading-related projects and assignments for building problem-solving skills.

Provide research opportunities to extend knowledge.

Ask mind-provoking questions before, during, and after reading.

Offer independent reading opportunities to extend thinking and knowledge related to the current topic.

DEVELOPING THE EAGER, FLUENT READER

There is no magic formula for developing an eager, fluent reader. We know from extensive research and effective practices, however, that certain elements create a learning community for the successful reader. These elements include the following.

Diagnosis and Assessment

- Know the individual student's strengths and needs.
- Learn how to use various reading assessment and diagnostic tools.
- Know how to match the diagnosis and assessment tools to the reader's needs.
- Explore the characteristics and behaviors of the individual reader.
- Identify specific reading problems and begin intervention procedures.
- Survey students to identify their interests and study habits related to reading.

Instruction

- Plan differentiated instruction for each individual's needs.
- Infuse reading comprehension, word attack skills, and vocabulary strategies into daily instruction.
- Expose the learner to enthusiastic, stimulating, expressive reading models.
- Scaffold instruction by introducing new skills within reach of the reader's success.
- Use meaningful activities to develop understanding before, during, and after each reading assignment.
- Use flexible grouping.
- Teach in the many ways the reader learns.
- Strategically plan time for the teacher to read aloud and for students to engage in silent and oral reading.
- Create intriguing experiences for the student to understand, use, and appreciate various genres.

Tools and Strategies

- Model each strategy in a purposeful manner.
- Teach the student how to select, personalize, and apply reading strategies.
- Show the student how to create and use mnemonic devices to memorize, use, adapt, and retain information for long-term use.
- Use a variety of strategies to teach a skill or concept.

Materials

- Provide a wide variety of materials and resources.
- Immerse the learner in challenging, high-interest reading materials.
- Select novel materials at the reader's level of understanding.
- Provide meaningful experiences so the student can make personal connections to text-related materials.

Environment

- Provide the least restrictive environment.
- Know the student's interests.
- Provide reading experiences that relate to the student's life.
- Keep the reader actively involved.
- Spark the learner's desire to read.
- Set high expectations with the "I can read!" feeling daily.
- Establish a challenging learning climate.
- Accept and honor individual diversity.
- Exude enthusiasm as a reading model.
- Create a team spirit for reading.

THE KEYS TO READING SUCCESS

Observe each student and assess the learner's unique situation. Assess the student before, during, and after reading. Chart the information. Look for students' reading behaviors. Diagnose and prescribe. Remember: Each student can learn to read, and you hold the key to each reader's success.

Reading Problems and Solutions

Solutions to reading problems begin with differentiated instruction. Students do not know how to overcome problems. When students have reading difficulties, the ability to comprehend subject information is hindered. These readers are usually embarrassed to read aloud. Students recognize their reading difficulties, and their confidence plummets. Their motivation for reading is hindered, and school performance suffers (Guthrie, 2008). Often these learners develop "don't care" attitudes. Struggling readers need solutions for diagnosed problems.

Figure 3.1 identifies common reading problems with suggested solutions. Remember, a perceived "problem" may in fact be the reader's best approach to oral or silent reading. Avoid using corrective measures that squelch the students' enthusiasm and desire to read. Cautiously analyze the reader's problem to find the best approaches and solutions.

FIVE VIEWS OF THE READER

Students bring a unique mix of personality traits, learning style preferences, intelligences, thinking styles, and reading strengths and weaknesses to the classroom culture. These affect the way a reader approaches learning and life each day. The following section offers five ways to think about your students as readers.

Learning Preferences

Demystifying and becoming aware of their own learning preferences will help students understand why they do the things they do as readers. Figure 3.2 is a

Figure 3.1	Reading Problems and Solutions	
Observable Characteristics	*Possible Problems*	*Suggested Solutions*
Reads one word at a time.	• Insecurity. • Visual perception. • Too much focus on decoding.	• Assign short phrases and passages. • Move pen light steadily over the words. • Check eyesight. • Use finger or marker to follow the lines. • Model fluent reading and ask the reader to mimic lines and phrases.
Words appear to move on the page while trying to read.	• Visual problem.	• Use colored transparency overlays. • Have sunglasses available with colored lenses (yellow, green, rose, blue). See if the student reads better with color. • Take reading notes on colored paper. • Tag notes with colored sticky tabs. • Recommend an ophthalmologist.
Is easily distracted.	• Does not complete tasks. • Accustomed to working alone.	• Needs a quiet place to read. • Needs directions given one step at a time. • Give specific praise for concentrating and staying on task.
Complains it is too quiet during independent reading.	• Cannot concentrate on reading in a quiet environment.	• Play background music. • Use personal music and headphones. • Ask specific questions from text to see that music improves concentration. • Encourage the student to select a comfortable place to read.
Lips move while reading.	• Developed this as a habit! • Needs to hear the words for comprehension. • Slows down the reading. • Is sometimes a word caller. • Hinders comprehension.	• Allow the student to lip-read, if it enhances comprehension. • Teach strategies to move faster across the lines for fluency. • Allow the student to use an interactive computer program. • Find the reader a quiet place to read away from other students. • Present "no lip reading" challenges using game formats.
Has trouble keeping place.	• Is easily distracted. • Has a visual/spatial deficiency. Cannot keep eyes on the reading line.	• Use fewer words on the page. • Check the lighting. • Give shorter assignments. • Use sticky notes to mark place. • Use a marker, pointer, or finger to follow words and stay on the line.
Reads but does not know what was read.	• Lacks comprehension skills. • Has not learned to focus. • Does not know the meaning of the words. • Does not understand directions.	• Use lead-ins or prompts to identify the purpose before reading. • Introduce vocabulary words in memorable ways. • Use short segments followed by quality discussions. • Use personal writing for rereading, rephrasing, and conversations. • Teach and model comprehension strategies. • Assess the reader's comprehension when someone reads the passage aloud.

personality profile offering a metaphor students can use to compare their learning preferences to objects such as a clipboard, microscope, puppy, or beach ball to identify their personality profiles.

Activity

1. Ask students to identify the objects that most closely symbolizes their preferences.

2. Have students rank the object preferences from 1 (most like them) to 4 (least like them).

3. Ask the students to write or tell why they made their top two choices.

When students understand their personality traits, they feel more encouraged to work within their favorite comfort zones.

Figure 3.2 The Object and You	
Clipboard	*Microscope*
<ul><li>Needs set procedures.</li><li>Works with clear, precise directions.</li><li>Seeks structure.</li><li>Learns with guided reading instruction.</li><li>Is productive in language experience.</li></ul>	<ul><li>Investigates and discovers.</li><li>Asks "Why?"</li><li>Needs experiments.</li><li>Focuses on the supporting details.</li><li>Enjoys research.</li><li>Digs for evidence.</li><li>Analyzes.</li></ul>
Puppy	*Beach Ball*
<ul><li>Needs a comfortable spot to read.</li><li>Is productive during group work.</li><li>Likes peer-to-peer tutoring.</li><li>Wants consensus.</li><li>Needs a safe climate.</li><li>Has a strong need to belong.</li><li>Wants everyone to be happy.</li></ul>	<ul><li>Needs a variety of reading materials.</li><li>Likes choices and flexibility.</li><li>Enjoys brainstorming.</li><li>Yearns for movement.</li><li>Enjoys using variation.</li><li>Thrives on active learning.</li><li>Seeks fun and excitement.</li><li>Needs effective hooks to focus.</li><li>Requires novelty.</li></ul>

Gardner's Multiple Intelligences

As mentioned in Chapter 1, Dr. Howard Gardner (1983) named multiple intelligences that are applicable to teaching and learning. These intelligences are not fixed but rather can be developed throughout our lives, so it is never too late to learn. Students' strongest intelligences are valuable pathways to overcoming weaknesses because lessons can be planned to utilize the learners' strongest intelligences to teach the reading skills. Figure 3.3 describes the characteristics of the intelligences as they relate to reading.

It is important for teachers to analyze the data and identify their own intelligences. Individuals naturally plan instruction that utilizes their three or four areas of strength. It should be remembered that many students in the class will not have the same strengths. Teachers must learn how to plan activities that are in their own weak areas to reach more students. Figure 3.4 on page 46 lists suggested activities for students with differentiated intelligences.

Figure 3.3 Multiple Intelligences in the Reading Classroom

Verbal/Linguistic	Musical/Rhythmic	Visual/Spatial	Logical/Mathematical
• Is a fluent reader. • Listens attentively. • Communicates in writing. • Links new and prior learning. • Debates issues. • Researches topics. • Applies vocabulary definitions. • Expresses a point of view. • Reads for pleasure. • Enjoys listening to others read. • Uses verbal mnemonics. • Chunks information. • Uses language to communicate effectively.	• Comprehends while reading with background music playing. • Looks for rhythmic patterns and poetry. • Spells words to a beat. • Attacks words by dividing them into syllables. • Creates songs, poems, jingles, chants, or raps to remember information. • Relates to the sound of a setting. • Reads with a rhythmic flow for fluency.	• Color codes and highlights. • Doodles. • Visualizes while reading. • Plots thinking on organizers. • Needs visual hooks. • Interprets, or draws pictures and graphics to understand text. • Uses art to express understanding. • Uses visual cues to comprehend. • Needs hands-on experiences with art media.	• Organizes information. • Outlines and classifies data. • Uses the scientific process. • Yearns to understand information sequence. • Learns with time lines. • Uses step-by-step procedures. • Reasons logically. • Needs clear, precise directions. • Learns trivia facts. • Enjoys logic-related games and puzzles. • Thinks abstractly and critically. • Learns with technology and gadgets. • Is a problem solver.

Bodily/Kinesthetic	Naturalist	Intrapersonal	Interpersonal
• Learns by role-playing. • Simulates events. • Creates artifacts. • Needs centers, labs, and hands-on learning opportunities. • Needs a comfortable spot of choice to read and work. • Can skillfully use the body. • Uses manipulatives to explore, learn, and discover. • Can skillfully use the body. • Can show or demonstrate it. • Needs to move to learn. • Responds to actions and feelings of characters.	• Yearns to discover with nature. • Intuitively relates and learns factual information about science and the surrounding world. • Explores habitats. • Conducts experiments. • Is a survivor. • Sees patterns in nature. • Copes and survives in most environments. • Relates to events and settings. • Responds to environmental issues and concerns. • Needs outdoor experiences.	• Works best independently. • Needs time to make personal application. • Enjoys opportunities for self-reflection. • Uses metacognitive thinking. • Needs time to process new learning independently. • Needs choice of a quiet space to read and work. • Establishes goals and accepts responsibilities. • Enjoys reading alone. • Learns with personal links and connections.	• Works best with others. • Enjoys partner reading. • Communicates with others. • Learns through interactions, such as text or literary talks. • Empathizes with struggling readers. • Needs to talk while learning. • Works well in flexible groups. • Enjoys discussions. • Is a social butterfly. • Understands others' feelings and emotions. • Needs interaction, conversations, and discussions. • Needs a listening ear.

Figure 3.4 Comprehension Tasks for Students

Verbal/Linguistic	Musical/Rhythmic	Logical/Mathematical	Visual/Spatial
• Read for understanding. • Write a summary. • Make a prediction. • Discuss relationships. • Vary genres. • Debate issues. • Take notes. • Write reflectively. • Write creatively. • Make a class presentation. • Research an issue. • Listen to text. • Answer questions.	• Create a topic theme song. • Create a musical game. • Make a CD, video, or tape. • Find background music. • Create setting sounds. • Write a song, rap, poem, cheer, or jingle. • Create a rhythmic pattern. • Memorize with a beat. • Use musical game show formats. • Match music with the mood of the passage.	• Create a time line. • Conduct a comparison. • Compare/contrast. • Develop a graph using data. • Develop a training guide. • Conduct an experiment. • Use a game show format. • Create a calendar of events. • Develop a sequence. • Use a matrix. • Be a problem solver. • Use the computer.	• Make a collage. • Videotape a scene. • Create a poster. • Paint a mural. • Invent a board game. • Sketch or draw. • Sequence scenes. • Draw a cartoon. • Use a graphic organizer. • Respond on a wipe-off board • Color code information. • Use visual imagery.

Bodily/Kinesthetic	Naturalist	Intrapersonal	Interpersonal
• Role-play. • Take on the role of a character. • Create story boards. • Build a model. • Create an adventure game. • Create a display. • Conduct experiments. • Investigate and explore.	• Relate information to nature. • Understand relationships. • Categorize. • Form a hypothesis. • Label and classify. • Predict. • Draw conclusions. • Apply survival skills. • Study the environment. • Understand science.	• Reflect. • Read independently. • Research. • Process the information. • Take notes. • Complete a project. • Question. • Use self-talk. • Study in preferred ways. • Use metacognitive thinking.	• Read and work with a partner. • Work with a small group. • Use cooperative learning. • Participate in choral reading. • Join a conversation circle. • Engage in a group project. • Interview. • Discuss your reading with others. • Participant in a mock trial. • Blog with a peer.

SOURCE: Adapted from Chapman C., & King, R. *Test Success in the Brain Compatible Classroom, Second Edition* Thousand Oaks, CA: Corwin 2008.

Sternberg's Triarchic Intelligences

This model focuses on three intelligences, known as the triarchic intelligences, which are key to success: analytical, practical, and creative (Sternberg & Grigerenko, 2007). Sternberg advises business groups to form decision-making teams with at least one member who is strong in each of these intelligences. Doing so creates a team with various ways of thinking for discussions and other tasks. This valuable idea can be applied by educators when designing plans to form groups for problem solving, cooperative learning, literacy studies, stations, and lab work. For example, select an analytical thinker to bring facts and research information into the discussion. Add a creative thinker to bring innovative ideas to the group. Include a practical thinker who can add workable, meaningful, and reasonable ideas. Figure 3.5 shows how learners apply the triarchic intelligences to reading.

Figure 3.5	Sternberg's Thinking as a Reader	
Practical	*Analytical*	*Creative*
• How can I use this information? • What is the author telling us here? • What will I learn from this? • This reminds me of _____.	• What are the facts? • What are the steps in the procedure? • What is the deeper meaning of this? • Examine the data.	• Predict what will happen next. • How can I apply this differently? • How can I use what I learned? • Brainstorm new ways to use the information.

Gregorc's Learning Styles and Reading

Dr. Anthony Gregorc (1985) made a huge impact on the way we think about learning styles. According to his theory, two variables are involved with the way individuals view the world, concrete and abstract. He also identified two avenues that we use to explore the way the world is viewed, a random or sequential order of things. Dr. Gregorc used these variables to create four learning styles.

Most educators work and plan activities using their two strongest thinking styles. However, it is often necessary for educators to use their weakest learning styles in their instruction to reach more students.

Analyze the combinations of learning styles shown in Figure 3.6 to identify the ways you think. Prioritize your thinking styles with #1 being the one you use most often and #4 the one you use least.

Figure 3.6	Gregorc's Learning Styles
Concrete/Sequential	*Abstract/Sequential*
• Desires to learn. • Uses lists, time lines, and procedural directions to create order. • Seeks details to support ideas. • Needs hands-on activities with manipulatives and experiments. • Thrives on personal engagement in reading-related experiences.	• Yearns for order and procedure. • Applies analytical thinking. • Uses visual imagery. • Adapts rational and logical thinking while reading. • Wants to investigate and analyze. • Needs time to process information read. • Seeks personal connections to reading.
Concrete/Random	*Abstract/Random*
• Is a divergent thinker. • Finds alternative ways to complete reading tasks. • Thrives on reading choices. • Understands the "big picture" quickly. • Learns through trial and error.	• Is flexible and spontaneous. • Reads best with a partner or group. • Interweaves feelings and emotions while reading. • Needs a nonthreatening environment. • Seeks variety. • Discovers the answer but may not know how or why.

McCarthy's 4MAT Model and Reading

In the 4MAT model, every individual has two strong types of thinking (McCarthy & McCarthy, 2006). Examining the 4MAT model shows that every effective lesson includes favorite zones and key components, including the following:

- An imagination component asking, "Why do we learn or need this?"
- An analytical component asking, "What are the important facts?"
- A commonsense component asking, "Is this the most effective activity to use during this time segment?"
- A dynamic, energetic component asking, "What creative idea can I use to teach this difficult concept?"

Figure 3.7 shows these four components as they relate to reading.

Figure 3.7	4MAT Models
Type I: The Imaginative Reader Asks "Why?"	*Type II: The Analytical Reader Asks "What?"*
• Uses feelings and reflections. • Asks questions. • Makes predictions and asks "What if . . . ?" • Discusses ideas. • Asks "Why?" while reading. • Questions content and reading purposes. • Seeks to understand author and character motives.	• Seeks facts. • Organizes information. • Analyzes and categorizes. • Works systematically. • Needs strong prereading lead-ins. • Learns with advanced organizers. • Seeks clear, specific purposes, directions, and expectations.

Type I: The Imaginative Reader Asks "Why?"	Type II: The Analytical Reader Asks "What?"
• Needs to make personal connections to reading. • Brainstorms effectively. • Seeks alternative solutions.	• Needs to receive interesting materials to be motivated to read. • Make judgments quickly. • Uses charts, graphs, lists, and graphic organizers. • Reflects and then acts.
Type III: The Commonsense Reader Asks "How?"	Type IV: The Dynamic Reader Asks "What can this become?"
• Seeks usability. • Wants practical applications. • Prefers to learn by trying things out. • Needs to be encouraged to experiment. • Asks "How can I apply this in my world?" • Prefers reality. • Readily compares and contrasts.	• Needs permission to create. • Enjoys freedom to risk with thinking. • Thinks outside the box. • Has an innate desire to work independently but works well in groups, too. • Believes in his or her own influence. • Avoids routine. • Enjoys activities related to personal growth and renewal.

ASSESSING AND DIAGNOSING THE READER

Assessment provides a clear, concrete way to identify what the reader needs to learn. The assessment process is ongoing. The student and the teacher monitor progress. The information determines future learning opportunities. Use the results of your assessments to plan differentiated lessons and grouping designs. Portfolios provide important assessment data to guide conferences with the reader, parent, or student support team.

Checklists are easy to use to track daily observations. Figure 3.8 on the next page presents a checklist to assess the status of the reader. Use this guide periodically throughout the year to watch the reader grow and use Figure 3.9 to record your observations. Note that some characteristics can be checked in each section.

Formal and Informal Assessment Tools

A wide variety of assessment tools are used before, during, and after the reading. These ongoing tools show progress, reveal places for interventions, and show where adjustments need to be made in instructional plans to meet the individual needs of each learner.

Use an effective blending or combination of formal and informal tools. Always remember that if an informal tool provides the information needed, use it instead of the formal tool. The assessment tools listed on page 51 in Figure 3.10 can be used throughout reading experiences.

Figure 3.8   Reader Status Checklist

Student _____   Class _____

Check all that apply.

Emerging Reader

____ Understands eye movement directions: left to right and top to bottom.
____ Uses picture clues.
____ Knows initial and final consonant sounds.
____ Knows the relationship of letters and words.
____ Demonstrates limited sight-word vocabulary.
____ Responds to some punctuation signs.
____ Exhibits behaviors that reflect insecurity and feelings of hopelessness.
____ Demonstrates inadequate comprehension skills.
____ Shows limited ability to decode unfamiliar words.
____ Displays negative attitudes toward reading assignments.

Successful Reader

____ Actively uses background knowledge as links to new information.
____ Is a confident reader.
____ Applies decoding skill.
____ Interprets text information at grade level.
____ Uses self-corrective reading strategies.
____ Engages in meaningful thinking while reading.
____ Remembers facts and general concepts.

Comprehending Fluent Reader

____ Derives meaning from reading passages.
____ Is able to retain and use the information.
____ Understands reading assignments.
____ Is an avid reader.
____ Uses context clues.
____ Has a broad sight vocabulary.
____ Makes self-corrections.
____ Decodes automatically.
____ Uses information in higher-order thinking.
____ Interprets purposes and meanings of reading activities.
____ Reads for enjoyment.
____ Enjoys reading in various genres.

Figure 3.9   Observation Grid for Reader Status Checklist

Observation 1	Observation 2	Observation 3
Date_____	Date_____	Date_____
_____ Emerging	_____ Emerging	_____ Emerging
_____ Successful	_____ Successful	_____ Successful
_____ Fluent	_____ Fluent	_____ Fluent
Comments	Comments	Comments
Observer_____	Observer_____	Observer_____

Figure 3.10 Formal and Informal Assessment Tools for Reading	
Formal Tools	*Informal Tools*
❑ Pretest/posttest	❑ Journaling
❑ Rubrics	❑ Signals
❑ Reading inventories	❑ Oral reading
❑ Fluency checks	❑ Response cards
❑ Running records	❑ Wipe-off boards
❑ Written responses	❑ Edit slips
❑ Checklist	❑ Bell-ringing activities
❑ Likert scales	❑ Discussions
❑ Surveys	❑ Question/answer time
❑ Inventories	❑ Literacy circles
❑ Anecdotal records	❑ Book studies
❑ Portfolios	❑ Games
❑ Formal test	❑ Observations
❑ Open-ended questions	❑ Station/center activities
❑ Multiple-choice questions	❑ Demonstrations
❑ Agree/disagree charts	❑ Homework
❑ True/false questions	❑ Turn and talk
❑ Notes	❑ Roar of crowd
❑ Conference	

Informal Reading Inventories (IRI)

Informal reading inventories (IRIs) are assessments designed to determine a student's reading level. The inventories identify ability level with sight words, oral reading, and comprehension.

Graded word lists and reading passages are used. The word lists and passages usually include all grade levels from preprimer to the eighth grade. The most effective IRIs are created by the teacher to meet the diverse needs of their readers, but IRIs are also commercially available for purchase.

Part I: Teacher-Made Vocabulary Level Assessment

Adapt the following guidelines to create an informal IRI to use in identifying a reader's vocabulary level:

1. Prepare a word list with 20 words you know the student can read with 100 percent accuracy. Prepare two more word lists that have 20 words at and above the student's expected reading level. Make two copies so the student has one to read while you record the correct responses and the types of errors made on the other copy.

2. Call on the student to read the list below his or her reading level.

3. Place a check mark by the words read correctly.

4. Mark incorrect words to indicate the type of error and make notes beside them.

5. If the student reads all words on the list or misses one word, move to the word list at the next level.

6. Stop when the student misses two words on a list and record the list's grade level.

7. Provide reading materials at the grade level indicated by this list.

Part II: Teacher-Made Comprehension Assessment

When using the IRI process, include the following steps:

1. Introduce the passage to motivate the student to read it.

2. Ask the student to answer explicit, detailed questions about the text content. These questions are designed to identify the reader's comprehension abilities.

3. Ask the student to answer questions that require implicit thinking about the passage. Here are some examples:

Summarize.	Draw conclusions.	Retell.
Relate to today's world.	List facts.	Write passage in own words.
Relate to self.	Evaluate the author's purpose.	Develop a critique for a magazine.

4. The learner writes a response or answers orally to demonstrate understanding of the text beyond the surface meaning.

Remember the following important points:

- *Use content text:* This demonstrates how the student approaches reading assignments.
- *Use high-interest material:* Higher comprehension occurs when the student possesses high interest in the material.
- *Look through the passage for difficult vocabulary words:* Choose wisely.

Cloze Process

A Cloze reading assessment checks the student's use of context clues for comprehension. Cloze procedures can be used to assess language ability, mastery of concepts, mastery of specialized vocabulary, or to test reading ability as it relates to the text.

In the Cloze process, the teacher rewrites a content passage with every tenth word omitted. The reader uses content background, prior knowledge, and thinking skills to fill in the blanks with the word that completes the meaning correctly. Variations for differentiation include leaving out fewer words or leaving out content vocabulary or concept words.

Surveys and Inventories

Learn as much about the students as possible. Effective assessments are ongoing and differentiated to meet the needs and the purposes of the learning. To personalize the reading culture, develop surveys, inventories, checklists, and rubrics to identify the students' needs in specific situations.

Surveys are valuable tools to assist teachers in getting to know the students' attitudes toward reading. Tune in to the student's thoughts, beliefs, interests, fears, and dreams. Use the surveys to personalize instruction and develop meaningful connections between the learner's life and the subject information. The surveys in Figures 3.11–3.15 can be adapted to all grade levels to survey student beliefs, interests, and environmental factors relevant to reading and learning.

Use Figure 3.13 in a student conference. Analyze and discuss the responses with the reader. Explain the terms *discomfort* and *comfort.* Ask the reader to place an *X* on each line to indicate his or her comfort level in each area.

Figure 3.11   Sample Interest Survey

1. My favorite way to spend time is . . .

2. I do not like to . . .

3. My favorite television show is . . .

4. My favorite movie is . . .

5. My favorite subject is . . .

6. The most difficult thing I do at school is . . .

7. The easiest thing I do at school is . . .

8. The reading materials I have at home are . . .

9. I spend the following number of hours a week doing each of these:

    _____ Watching television   _____ Listening to the radio

    _____ Talking on the telephone   _____ Working on homework

    _____ Playing a sport   _____ Spending time with friends

    _____ Other

10. The following people read to me:

11. Currently I am reading . . .

12. I like to read when . . .

13. My favorite author is . . .

14. I enjoy reading about . . .

15. I enjoy listening to stories about . . .

Figure 3.12   Student Beliefs Survey

 1. If you had a million dollars, how would you spend it?

 2. Name five things you would like to do now or later in your life.

 3. How do you like to spend your free time?

 4. What are your hobbies and interests?

 5. What do you read?

 6. What do you do after school?

 7. What is the first thing you think when someone asks you to read aloud?

 8. How do you feel when you have a reading assignment to complete alone?

 9. What are two of the best books you have heard or read?

10. What is the worst experience you have had with reading?

11. What are two of the best experiences you have had with reading?

Figure 3.13   Where Am I as a Learner?

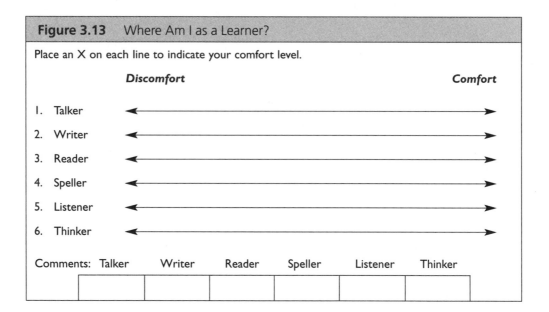

Place an X on each line to indicate your comfort level.

	Discomfort					Comfort
1. Talker						
2. Writer						
3. Reader						
4. Speller						
5. Listener						
6. Thinker						

Comments:	Talker	Writer	Reader	Speller	Listener	Thinker

Additional Student Surveys

Figures 3.14 and 3.15 offer some additional surveys. Gather student information three or four times during the year because hobbies, interests and personal situations may change. Refer to the responses to develop customized instructional plans for the reader. Add other areas to the surveys as needed.

Figure 3.14   Student Interest Survey

Student Name _____   Date _____

Place a plus sign (+) beside three things you like to do most after school.
Place a minus sign (−) beside three of your least favorite things to do after school.

	Work on a computer.		Play games outside.
	Talk on the phone.		Go to a movie.
	Watch television.		Practice for a game with my team.
	Read a book.		Take dance lessons.
	Work for pay.		Take special classes.
	Visit with my friends.		Spend time with my parents.
	Other: _____		Other: _____

Describe your favorite hobbies, pastimes, or interests.

1	2	3

Give reasons for choosing each of your least favorite ways to spend time.

1	2	3

Figure 3.15   Home Environment Survey

1. Do you have a specific time to study at home?

2. Do you have a room of your own?

3. Do you have access to a computer?

4. How much time do you spend watching TV each day?

5. How much time do you spend on computers?

6. How much time do you spend on the phone or texting?

7. Do your parents keep track of your work activities at school?

8. What kinds of reading materials are in your home?

Using Assessments Effectively

Effective teachers plan, plan, and further plan reading experiences using assessment data collected before, during, and after units of study. During lessons, the data are used to monitor the progress of individuals, small groups, and the total class. The data is collected through personal notes, written tests, checklists, and observation tools. Students demystify learning when they understand their strengths and areas of need (Levine, 2002). Levine says, "Kids need to know themselves and they need to know what to work on to help themselves" (p. 278).

Provide activities that permit students to interact with ideas. Actively engage readers in thoughtful activities and experiences related to the content information and resources. Make multiple formats available to entice readers within their ability range and interest areas.

Figure 3.16 is an example of an Individual Learning Plan.

Portfolio Assessment

The possibilities [of portfolios] are limitless, and the feedback is illuminating. After all, feedback is the food of champion readers.

—Fogarty (2007, p. 46)

Portfolios contain samples of the student's work. They help learners, teachers, and parents monitor the reader's progress through the collected work samples. The benefits of portfolio assessment are many, including

- Providing daily evidence of ongoing needs and growth.
- Empowering the learner with learning strategies and skills.
- Increasing the student's personal responsibility in learning.
- Stressing self-efficacy, the "I can do!" feeling.
- Teaching the student to be self-reflective.
- Providing avenues for self-analysis and self-improvement.
- Guiding the learner to higher levels of thinking.
- Providing evidence of growth from initial to current entries.
- Teaching strategies for self-evaluation and peer critiques.
- Generating genuine pride in accomplishments.
- Showcasing success.

Figure 3.16   Individual Learning Plan

Student Name _____   **Grade** _____   **Date** _____

Class _____   **Reading Level** _____

Gardner's Multiple Intelligences

Place a plus sign (+) beside areas of strength. Place a minus sign (–) beside areas of need.

___V/L ___M/R ___L/M ___B/K ___V/S ___N ___I/A ___ I/er

Comments_____

_____

_____

Sternberg's Triarchic Intelligences

Place a plus sign (+) beside areas of strength. Place a minus sign (–) beside areas of need.

___ Analytical   ___ Practical   ___ Creative

Comments_____

_____

_____

Learning Styles

Place a plus sign (+) beside areas of strength. Place a minus sign (–) beside areas of need.

___ Auditory   ___ Visual   ___ Tactile-kinesthetic

Comments _____

_____

Other Personal Preferences for Reading Experiences:

_____   _____   _____

Strengths _____   _____   _____

Needs _____   _____   _____

Interests/Hobbies _____   _____   _____

Independent Reading Materials:

Instructional Strategies:

Instructional Materials:

Showcase Scoring

Teachers and students enjoy developing and using a scoring rubric for portfolios. The rubric sets the expectations for an assignment from the onset of the activity and leads to final evaluation. Here is an example:

5   Above and Beyond
    Completed more activities
        than those required.
    Completed and organized all
        assignments.
    Turned in the assignment on time.

4   On Track
    Completed assignments.
    Organized the work.
    Completed the work on time.

3   Not Quite There
    Is missing one or two pieces.
    Few pieces are organized.
    Assignment is one day late.

2   Thrown Together
    Three or more pieces are missing.
    There is little organization.
    Assignment is two days late.

1   A "No-Show" Effort
    Did not try.
    There are few examples of ability.
    Assignment is more than two days
        late.

THE GRADING DILEMMA

One of the biggest problems faced by teachers in a differentiated classroom is knowing how and when to assess the student for grades. Often a teacher thinks, "If the student is working at his own level, then I am meeting his needs, and his grades are very high, usually As and Bs." This is the right picture because it acknowledges and celebrates growth. However, it is the wrong picture if the work is below grade level.

The other way to view this dilemma is that teachers must teach to state and federal mandates to prepare students to meet those standards. Thus, some of the learner's grades should reflect a comparison with students in the same grade level across the country.

Combining Assessments

In the differentiated classroom, a combination of assessments gives a more complete picture of the student's performance for the final grade. Try the following assessment combinations:

1. *Assign grades that reflect the reader's accomplishments and areas of need.* Consider the student's efforts, creativity, and ability to stay with a task when determining the grade. If a reader is graded using a perspective that does not focus on the individual's strengths, the teacher does not have a true picture of the learner's ability. A reader's preference for learning has a major impact on his or her success with a concept or skill. When the reader's ability is below grade level, use an assessment tool to

gather data using the student's strongest areas. For example, if the reader has difficulty with structural analysis but exhibits strength in the musical rhythmic area, ask the learner to create a jingle, rap, or rhyme to demonstrate knowledge as the assessment.

2. *For a formal assessment, administer the same pretest and posttest to determine the reader's growth in learning.* The results reflect the student's knowledge and skill level at the beginning of the learning, and these tests readily evaluate progress at the end of the study. This approach also identifies areas of strengths and needs. The data are used in planning the next unit of study.

3. *Administer assessment pieces at the reader's grade level to compare his or her ability to other students in the class.* The results indicate the reader's standing in relation to classmates. They also show how the learner meets the criteria or standard set for that grade level, class, or subject. Use formal or informal assessments throughout the learning. When the study ends, the grade is based on evaluation of the student's work as reflected in the portfolio.

When the teacher combines these three forms of assessment, a clearer picture of the reader's ability is revealed. The final grade is assigned with a portfolio as evidence to support it. This provides a more complete view of the reader's accomplishments, weaknesses, and growth. In the words of Rona F. Flippo (2001):

> The real common ground includes the understanding that reading is not simple, and there are no simple answers or solutions that can be applied to all children and situations: Instead of simplistic answers, solutions, and one-way-only approaches, the common wisdom of the field point [sic] to the need to allow teachers the flexibility to select the methods, approaches, and materials to fit the particular child and situation. Reading development and instruction is far too complex and involves far too many variables to try to simplify and prescribe it for all students in all situations. (p. 178)

SUMMARY

Each reader's knowledge base, learning styles, intelligences, and attitude play a major role in success with each reading activity. When the teacher identifies the learner's background knowledge and the many ways he or she learns, it is easier to plan and customize reading activities.

Design each lesson using differentiated instruction to give the reader successful experiences. Before the pace of instruction is set, consider the individual's developmental readiness for the specific skill. If a skill is too difficult, the student is frustrated. If the skill is too easy, the reader is bored. The challenge is to orchestrate each lesson so the skill is within the reader's level of success.

Each reader's diverse needs become evident through behaviors in daily activities. Emotional reactions during reading experiences indicate feelings related to the passage. Always remember that past experiences usually determine the student's negative or positive response to reading activities. Keep a log of observable behaviors and use the information as an integral part of the learner's assessment.

Use a variety of assessment tools to gather information. Use the data to diagnose the reader's problems and prescribe solutions. Use the reader's strengths to address weaknesses. For example, if a learner has difficulty comprehending the text and excels in art, encourage this reader to draw a picture to illustrate the information. Remember: A learner who is strong in one area needs regular opportunities to grow and nurture that strength. For example, if the learner is a fluent, comprehending reader, provide opportunities for in-depth investigations and explorations in a related aspect of the current study to extend and enrich the student's knowledge.

Know the characteristics, strengths, and needs of the reading characters in your classroom. Use this knowledge to create an environment that builds on interests, generates excitement, supports effort, and encourages and inspires each reader.

DIFFERENTIATED MODELS AND STRATEGIES OF READING **4**

THE DIFFERENTIATED MODELS OF READING DISCUSSED IN this chapter provide a framework for planning instruction. Each model is designed for immediate use in the classroom within the content area curriculum. Adapt the suggestions and guidelines to your teaching strategies. Choose the reading model to match your students' needs and enhance their reading skills.

ADJUSTABLE ASSIGNMENT MODEL

Adjustable assignments are used to plan for the teaching of one topic, standard, skill, objective, or essential question to students who are on multiple levels of learning. The standard, skill, or concept is identified. An appropriate preassessment identifies the background knowledge and experiences of the students in relation to the new learning. In most classes, an analysis of the data reveals three distinct groups.

- One group has the proper background and is ready for the grade-level standard.

- Another group lacks the proper background knowledge or experiences for the lesson. This group has gaps in learning that hinder the ability to fully understand the standard. The teacher plans instruction to intervene and fill in the learning gaps for these students. Of course, all deficiencies cannot be addressed, so select the skill that fills in the most important missing piece for the standard. In Chapman and King's *Differentiated Instructional Management* (2008), this process is referred to as curriculum rewinding.

- The third group has the proper background and has mastered the standard. These readers need assignments that enrich, challenge, and fast-forward their learning.

When a teacher knows specific information about a student's background knowledge on a topic, appropriate actions are planned so all readers grow in learning.

With adjustable assignments (see Figure 4.1 on the next page), the learner begins with current knowledge and skills and moves into identified areas of deficiency. Analyze the needs of students, than make strategic plans for individuals and specific groups. Design activities and tasks that produce growth and improvement for each reader.

Figure 4.1   Adjustable Assignment Model

Standard _____

Preassessment Tool _____

C		How will I teach each group?	
B	Which	skill does each group need to	learn next?
A	What	does each group know about	this topic?
	High Degree of Mastery	Approaching Mastery	Beginning

SOURCE: Adapted from Chapman & King, 2008.

See Figure 4.2 for an adjustable model showing levels of readiness for research assignments.

Figure 4.2   Adjustable Model for Research

Has resources and uses them effectively. Clearly defines and expands the topic. Works independently and productively. Work reflects creativity. Uses accurate information.	Uses two or more sources to locate information. Stays on topic. Needs little assistance. Has some awareness of purpose. Shows some organization.	Uses one source for given topic. Ongoing assistance is required. Has inadequate awareness of purpose. Lacks skills to organize thoughts.
High Degree of Mastery	*Approaching Mastery*	*Beginning*

SOURCE: Adapted from Gregory & Chapman, 2007.

CURRICULUM-COMPACTING MODEL

To meet the needs of high-end learners in a particular topic, Dr. Joseph Renzulli designed the curriculum-compacting model (Renzulli, Leppien, & Hayes, 2000; see also Tomlinson, 1999, 2001).

Many readers study and explore the world as researchers and discoverers of information. If students are experts on a topic or have mastered a standard or skill, they need a special plan so they, too, grow in knowledge. These students deserve an alternative with an exemption for the grade-level tasks. Here are some examples:

- Students work with an agenda assignment containing a list of challenging tasks.
- Students who have mastered the vocabulary words receive a more difficult list to broaden their vocabulary.
- Students who read at a higher level go to another classroom for reading instruction. The reading teacher is responsible for the grade.

CENTERS AND STATIONS MODEL

Add centers and stations, labs, cooperative groups, and personalized instruction to your classroom. Design periods of time for hands-on experiences to make learning happen. Students work independently and in small groups at manipulative stations, experiencing content in meaningful ways. This approach allows students to take control of their learning.

Examples of Reading Stations, Centers, or Learning Zones

Stations are set up as an assembly-line process, with students working in each area. Center activities can be leveled according to difficulty. This way, the students are assigned to the center or station based on preassessment data that identify individual needs.

The stations can be designed for student selection so they choose a place to work. This gives readers responsibility and ownership in learning.

Here are examples of hands-on centers or stations to use with all subjects.

Book-making station	Manipulatives	Resource library
Center bulletin boards	Problem-solving puzzles	Skills centers
Computer games	Reading nook	Tubs with manipulatives
Folder games	Reading response center	Vocabulary-building center

PROJECT-BASED MODELS

Project-based learning fosters in-depth studies about a unit. Everyone is given the same assignment, guidelines, rubric, and time line, but the topics and products vary. For example, students receive an assignment to create a travel brochure with the same criteria and grading rubric, but each brochure will have a different appearance, because different destinations are depicted. In this example, students may use any media to design their brochures.

Projects can be assigned in different ways, depending on the model used:

- In a multiple intelligences model, the lists of the possible project assignments are created around targeted intelligences, with students choosing projects they prefer.
- In a student choice contract model, the student presents a proposal to the teacher for a project. This can include the idea, reasons, procedure, and product. The contract is approved by the teacher. Guidelines, criteria, and rubrics are set by the teacher to establish standards and expectations for the project.

Here are some questions to consider:

- Will the project be an ongoing part of the instruction in one or more content areas?
- Will the project be a culminating activity to show what the student has learned within a specific area of focus or topic?
- Will the project be a shared home and school commitment?
- Will the project be worthwhile?

Here are some factors to consider when making project assignments:

- *Experience appropriateness:* Will the student be able to process and utilize the information and resources?
- *Content:* How will the project be used to extend the learning process in a particular study area?

Remember to plan peer-to-peer conferences throughout the project process so the student is held accountable for progress on assignments along the time line. This encourages individuals to pace their work on the project instead of waiting until the last minute to complete it.

PROBLEM-SOLVING MODEL

The reader, a small group, or a class can identify a problem to solve or be given a problem. It is usually related to the school, local community, or world. The problem can be assigned to the total group (T), a student working alone (A), partners (P), or small groups (S) using the TAPS model. For instance, in one classroom the students stated that a traffic light was needed near the local community sports center. The teacher arranged for the students to work with a traffic engineer to gather information on regulations and requirements for installing a traffic light. The students created charts and graphs to share the information gathered.

The teacher arranged for the class to visit the intersection to gather more data. Students shared the collected data with the traffic engineer. Today that intersection has a traffic light.

INDEPENDENT CHOICE READING MODEL

Independent reading time provides students with opportunities to choose fact or fiction to read. A supply of ready resources in the students' areas of interest is available in the classroom for selection during this time.

Some teachers allow students to bring materials from the media center, the local library, or home. These materials may need adult approval. When the reading materials are assembled, the classroom shelves contain a variety of information relevant to the current topic, such as the examples in the following list.

Factual information	Readers' ability levels
Fictional accounts	Reference materials
Illustration booklet	Students' areas of interest
Materials written in different genres	

Students need specific times to choose books and materials for independent reading. This is an ideal way to encourage reading for pleasure because students know they can find something on the resource shelf they are anxious to read.

GUIDED READING MODEL

The purpose of guided reading is to empower students with independent reading skills and strategies they will automatically use to interpret texts and related materials. Guided reading activities are teacher-directed learning opportunities. Conduct guided reading with a total class, a small group, or one student.

Engage each student in sharing and discussing ideas in the passage. Ask comprehension questions to determine the students' understanding of the reading. Use questions to elicit responses that require literal, inferential, and evaluative comprehension. Present the skills through modeling, explanations, examples, and discussions during this special reading time.

In most classrooms, the guided reading groups form with students of similar needs. While one group works with the teacher, other students work on specific reading skills in centers, with partners, or independently. As the students' needs and strengths change, so do the individuals who make up each group.

The Teacher's Role in Guided Reading

The teacher leads the students through reading passages modeling appropriate skills and strategies.

1. *Activate prior knowledge.* Use lead-ins, essential questions, graphics, music, or props to activate memories linking prior knowledge and experiences to the new learning. Here are some examples:
   - What do you think this is about?
   - What is going to happen?

- Today we are going to . . .
- How many of you remember . . . ?
- Remember a time when . . . ? Tell us about it.
- Look at this picture. What does the picture tell you?
- Do the topics and subheadings remind you of an experience you have had or something you have read? Tell me about it.
- What do you think when you hear this music?

2. *Teach vocabulary* words, standards, and skills related to the passages.

3. *Monitor readers* and respond strategically with cues, prompts, and assistance. These aids further refine understanding of the passage.

4. *Teach students how to monitor* their comprehension and how to fix a breakdown in understanding.

5. *Model specific reasoning processes* used by effective readers to construct meaning of the text. Give students step-by-step directions to follow when completing a task. Talk through the thinking process to demonstrate how to control thinking while reading.

Sample Model for a Guided Reading Session

1. Choose the reading selection and identify the group, using flexible grouping.

2. Match the text to the instructional level of the students.

3. Get ready for reading.
   - Assess to identify the students' background knowledge.
   - Arouse interest with hooks and anticipatory carrots.
   - Set purposes.

4. Introduce the new vocabulary and skills in novel ways (see Chapter 5).
   - Analyze the structure of the word.
   - Learn the word and its meaning as used in the text.

5. Make predictions.

6. Introduce the passage with prereading activities.
   - Discuss the title and subheading.
   - Preview graphics, charts, and pictures.
   - Present the essential questions and purposes.
   - Announce the focus for learning.

7. Read the passage.
   - Assign short passages. Some assignments call for note taking.
   - Provide time for independent reading.
   - Intervene with assistance as needed.

8. Discuss and develop comprehension skills (see Chapter 7).
   - Discuss answers to questions and facts discovered.
   - Review organization and sequence.
   - Redefine the purpose.

9. Reread orally with a small group, partner, or total group if oral reading skills are weak.

10. Use the information learned to differentiate assignments for individual need.

11. Employ intelligence and modality tools to customize activities and assignments.

12. Use follow-up activities to teach, practice, and review skills, concepts, and strategies.

13. Locate additional information and sources.

14. Use learned information in creative displays, portfolios, reports, or presentations.

Assessment of Guided Reading

Use a checklist similar to Figure 4.3 to assess the learner's progress.

Figure 4.3 Assessment of Guided Reading			
Student's Name _____ Teacher's Name _____ Date _____			
Learner Skill	Not Yet	Developing	Consistent
Reads orally with expression.			
Knows the vocabulary.			
Recognizes and uses punctuation to guide reading.			
Demonstrates understanding of text.			
Retells the story or information.			
Makes predictions.			
Interprets characters' feelings.			
Makes inferences.			
Comments			

LANGUAGE EXPERIENCE MODEL

In a language experience activity, the teacher selects a content-related topic. The students are given a prompt or questions about the topic to elicit oral responses.

As a student responds, the teacher writes exactly what the individual says, word for word. This activity demonstrates the writing-reading connection. Students gather near the teacher to see their words recorded and read. Chart paper is recommended, because it is easy to handle, display, move, and revisit as needed. It is important for students to see the chart, board, paper, or computer screen as their words are recorded.

During a language experience activity, learners observe letters forming words, the words making sentences, and sentences creating paragraphs. The teacher repeats the student's words, modeling how the spoken words appear in the form of writing. Often students do not understand that the words they say are the same words written on the paper. The teacher explicitly demonstrates that spoken words are now in a written form. Read each phrase as it is written. Read each sentence as it is completed. Invite students to read specific phrases and sentences. Lead the group in rereading the recorded information.

Learners may know what they want to say but have difficulty writing it. Language experience activities teach students the value of writing their words as they say them. Each experience demonstrates the writing and reading connection through content lessons.

The language experience is a vital tool to use because students can read their own words in writing and receive teacher guidance, which students often need while reading. The language experience is effective with an individual, a small group, or a total class.

Language Experiences in the Lower Grades

The teacher usually selects the topic for a language experience in the lower grades. The class can choose a title before the writing begins or select a catchy, clever title when the activity is completed.

The student gives the information to the teacher orally. The teacher writes the sentence, saying the name of each letter of the word as it takes form on the chart. The student repeats the letter's name. For example, if a student's sentence begins with the letter *T*, the teacher says, "Capital *T*," while writing it. The student repeats it, saying, "Capital *T*." When the letters form a word, the teacher and the student say the word together. For example, the teacher says, "T-h-e spells *the*," and the group repeats it.

Using this method, the teacher reinforces each letter's name, the recognition of every word, and the connection of words to create sentences. When a sentence is complete, the teacher brings attention to each word by using a pointer while reading the sentence to the listening students. The readers repeat the sentence. As each learner becomes more proficient with letter recognition, spelling, and reading, individual progress is evident. Students join their voices with the teacher's as the letters and words appear in the writing. Upon completion of a chart, the class and the teacher read the entire story, passage, or list together.

Language Experiences in the Upper Grades

Language experience activities are effective for conveying topic information in the upper grades. A chart, blackboard, overhead, or computer projection screen is used to record student responses during a small-group or class discussion. The teacher reads each word, sentence, or phrase after writing it. This repetition reinforces word recognition and correct spelling.

Any time a teacher records a student's words, it is a language experience. This technique records student responses to questions during class discussions. For example, students realize that as they speak, the teacher is scripting their words. When responding to an open-ended question on a test, learners realize the need to write thoughts in words as they would say them orally. Often a student knows the answers but does not know how to transfer thoughts and information to tests. Language experience activities develop metacognitive skills the reader needs to record thoughts in all academic activities.

Teachers often misinterpret the students' information as they are writing it. The teacher continually asks for clarification, because the student may not volunteer to correct the teacher if thoughts are recorded incorrectly.

The teacher also encourages the student to give further explanations. If the information is not clear, the student can be asked to respond to probing questions. Encourage the student to use explanations that clarify the previous statement. Here are some examples of questions to use for clarification.

- Tell me more.
- What part do you not understand?
- Explain this idea.
- What does this mean?

Create an adjustable assignment similar to that shown in Figure 4.4 for a language experience activity. Identify and record the student's knowledge base in the lower section. Record what your students need next above the line.

Figure 4.4 Adjustable Assignment for Language Experience

• Can write and read the story. • Is a leading contributor to the language experience process. • Has a strong knowledge base of language and sentence construction. • Spells the word before the teacher writes it. • Is a fluent, comprehending reader.	• Contributes to the story or topic. • Recognizes and knows how to spell most common words. • Reads most of the words without assistance.	• Repeats letters and words after the teacher. • Reads a few words without assistance.
High Degree of Mastery	*Approaching Mastery*	*Beginning*

SOURCE: Adapted from Gregory & Chapman, 2007.

SHARED READING MODEL

During shared reading experiences, everyone has an individual copy of the passage selected for the activity. The students gather around the teacher. Selecting the right passage is important to making this activity successful. The pupils follow the words as the teacher reads to them. Students who know how to read some words join in the reading. During the shared reading, the teacher provides needed word prompts and cues. The students participate in a rereading and retelling activity. This approach is recommended for beginning readers and English-language learners of all ages.

Use these suggested guidelines for shared reading:

1. Choose an appropriate selection with interesting, intriguing topic information.

2. Use books with predictable language, such as a rhyme, rhythmic text, or repetitive phrases.

3. Begin with an exciting hook to build interest in the reading.

4. Let the students make predictions about the selection.

5. Read the passage aloud.

6. Discuss the selection.
   - Ask students to give the information in their own words.
   - Elicit and confirm predictions.
   - Describe the details and valuable descriptive information.

7. Repeat the reading using various reading designs.
   - Assign parts for the students to read with the teacher.
   - Ask students to join in the parts they are able to read.

8. Provide a follow-up experience.

During shared reading experiences, students see the connection between written and spoken forms of language. They learn to read a passage from beginning to end and see that print runs from left to right and from top to bottom. Students hear and see reading modeled. Listeners hear the story read with expression and fluency. As the book or selection is read again, students further develop their listening and sight vocabularies. The discussions and follow-up activities teach readers that meaning comes from print.

READ-ALOUD MODEL

Read-aloud experiences give students of all ages the opportunity to hear the sounds and rhythms of the language. Each student needs to be read to every day. Jim Trelease, author of *The Read-Aloud Handbook* (2001), says if every person were read to orally every day from birth until age 21, we would have a literate world.

Read aloud to students each day. Make this a special, daily routine in all classrooms, in all subjects, and in all grade levels. Choose passages that relate to the topic of study or a high-interest area. (See Figure 4.5 for suggested sources of read-aloud materials.) The read-aloud time gives the student the opportunity to see and hear a reading model. When adults read aloud, they need to show passion for the piece through their emotions, voice inflections, and feelings. Relationships of letters to words, words to phrases, phrases to sentences, and sentences to paragraphs are better understood when the listener views the printed material as it is read aloud.

Figure 4.5 Suggested Read-Aloud Materials

Chapter books	Newspapers	Trivia	Riddles
Picture books	School newsletters	Quotes	Announcements
Fiction	Magazines	Sayings	Biographical sketches
Textbooks	Brochures	Brain teasers	Lyrics
Journals	Sports tidbits	Cartoons	Poetry
Reference entries	Movie reviews	Play scripts	Comic books
Articles	Spotlight a hero	Current events	Jokes
Game statistics	Weather reports	Fashion tips	Advertisements
Topic references	Editorials	News flashes	Travel Brochures

FOUR-BLOCK MODEL

The four-block planning format teaches reading in an organized manner, covering specific components, such as vocabulary development, guided reading, independent reading, and writing. Each block consists of a 60- to 90-minute period. A reading component is taught during each allotted block of time.

Some instruction is conducted with the total group. For example, the entire class may need to hear the directions and the introductory hook. On the other hand, some reading skills and strategies develop as the student works alone. For example, students need time to work alone to create their own interpretations of the information read. At other times, they find a comfortable place to work with a reading partner. Often instruction leads to small-group work. For example, the teacher may lead a group in a guided reading lesson. Guided reading sessions provide opportunities to model reading, teach skills, assess, and apply thinking skills in differentiated group scenarios.

Preassess the students to identify their background knowledge related to the standard. Design flexible grouping to tap into preferences and the potential of diverse learners. The four-block method is a structured way to plan reading instruction strategically. With appropriate activities in each quadrant (see Figure 4.6), fluent, comprehending readers develop through well-planned, meaningful lessons.

Figure 4.6 Four-Block Planning	
Vocabulary Development	*Guided Reading*
Design activities to . . . • introduce, assess, and review vocabulary words. • decode and pronounce words. • work with structural analysis clues. • apply phonics automatically. • master sight words. • study word origins. • learn and apply meanings. • teach mnemonics and hooks for learning new words. • use new words in daily conversations. • engage intelligences, learning styles, and interests. • entice and challenge with word games.	*Design activities to . . .* • provide a wide range of fiction and nonfiction materials related to the topic. • model and teach comprehension strategies and skills. • learn how to use context clues. • use a text or multiple copies of a trade book or literature (fiction, nonfiction). • teach reading skills and tools. • check for understanding of passages. • read in various genres related to the topic. • use different levels of thinking to check for understanding. • use explicit, inference, and evaluative questions. • develop the ability to identify the author's purpose, main ideas, and supporting details. • identify problems and find solutions.
Independent Reading	*Writing*
Design activities to . . . • learn how to select and read personal reading materials. • practice specific reading skills. • develop an eager, fluent reader. • develop opportunities to read a variety of materials. • allow reading text assignments alone or with others. • allow reading at one's own pace. • enhance comprehension and interpret information. • create a personal fit for success. • read materials in areas of interest.	*Design activities to . . .* • respond to and interpret in written form the information read. • record thoughts on graphic organizers. • express points of view and draw conclusions. • use different types of writing to respond to reading. • use various genres. • provide reflections. • engage in self-analysis. • process information. • critique, analyze, or summarize. • provide choice.

FROM MODELS TO IMPLEMENTATION

The following differentiated instructional strategies include agendas, cubing, response books, graphic organizers, and choice boards to use with content material. The flexibility of each activity provides options to meet the reader's individual needs during the implementation of a specific reading model.

Agendas and Menus

An agenda is a list of tasks for an individual or a small group of students to complete during independent work time. In many schools, this list is referred to as a "menu." Often while students work on their agendas, a teacher works with a small group, assisting students or assessing individual learners.

An agenda is an organizational tool for planning instruction that allows all students to work at their own levels. An agenda can be used with students of any age in any subject area across the curriculum. Small groups may have the same items on their assignment lists. The agenda is tailored to the individual's need and knowledge base.

The agenda for individual students or small groups may be presented in a folder or displayed in a designated area of the classroom. The tasks are determined from a data analysis of a preassessment. Before the work, begins the students know the due date for the completed tasks. Tasks on the list should be completed in a specified time. For example, during a unit of study, students are assigned specific tasks related to a standard. Before the work begins, the students know the due date for the completed tasks. Students who share similar knowledge, interests, or ability levels work though the same tasks.

The teacher and the students assess progress. As part of the information in the folder, the students are given an agenda log (see Figure 4.7) or an agenda checklist (Figure 4.8). The student can record each entry at the end of a work session.

Figure 4.7   Agenda Log

Item and Date	Today I	I need help on . . .	Completion Date	Comments

Figure 4.8   Agenda Self-Check

Student_____ Topic, Subject, or Unit_____

Date of Assignment_____ Due Date_____

TASK	A	B	C	D
Task or assignment				
Beginning work date				
Completion date				
What I learned				
Request for assistance				
Concerns and questions				
Comments				

Check Points	Identification _____ Signature _____ Date _____
Identification S: Self C: Classmate P: Parent T: Teacher	Identification _____ Signature _____ Date _____
	Identification _____ Signature _____ Date _____
	Identification _____ Signature _____ Date _____

Why Use Agendas?

- *Pacing:* Agendas teach the reader how to organize task sessions, use time wisely, and complete tasks within a set period. The teacher allots adequate time for the student to work effectively and efficiently on each task.

- *Sequence:* The student determines the order in which to complete the agenda items. One learner may complete the easiest tasks first, while another may complete difficult tasks first.

- *Independence:* Agendas foster independence. A student who is working on an agenda accepts personal responsibility for completing the assignment.

- *Time on-task:* Agenda assignments provide independent practice with and growth in the individual skills indicated as needs by the assessment data. This approach eliminates busywork and fosters efficient and quality use of time.

How Are Agendas Used?

- The teacher assigns all tasks.
- The teacher assigns some tasks, and the student chooses others from a choice board or a list of agenda ideas (see Figure 4.9).

Here's an example of how this can work. The teacher assigns one to three tasks and allows students to choose two to four tasks from a choice board. Students may design an activity related to the topic and submit it for teacher approval.

Reading Learning Zones, Centers, and Stations

Stations (see Figure 4.10 on page 76) are an important addition to any differentiated classroom. Preassess well so you know which activity each student needs next. Strategically plan activities that do the following:

- Teach the needed information. Select activities at the knowledge-base levels to teach the addressed standards, concepts, and skills. Also, remember to level the activities and tasks with a blending of grade-level and high-challenge opportunities.

- Intrigue students and hold their interest, making them anticipate and yearn to engage in the activity.

- Provide age-appropriate and stimulating tasks that intrigue and challenge the mind.

- Provide student-focused tasks that can be completed without adult supervision.

Try This Management Tip!

Color-code folders and activities to identify the knowledge-base or background level (see Figure 4.11 on page 76). Assign readers a yellow, red, or green activity to work on a standard, skill, or concept at the appropriate level to meet the individual's needs (Chapman & King, 2008).

Figure 4.9 Agenda Ideas

Reading-Related Material	Computer Activities	Art Project	Logical Thinking	Reenactment	Hands-on Learning	Listening and Viewing
• Take notes on the material. • Plot the information on a graphic organizer. • Create a fact sheet about the passage. • Identify vocabulary words and meanings. • Create a sequence board with the information. • Design a poster with the new information.	• Gather research on the Web. • Create a PowerPoint presentation. • Create a Word document about the topic. • Solve a crossword or other word puzzle. • Play an educational game. • Use a computer program related to the facts. • Design a graphic. • Use a word processor to add the facts in another genre.	• Create a collage or mobile. • Design a mural. • Make a diorama. • Develop a poster. • Sculpt a character. • Build a setting. • Illustrate the information or procedure. • Develop an editorial cartoon. • Draw the scene of the event. • Illustrate the meanings of a vocabulary word or concept.	• Write what you learned. • Develop a time line. • Write the step-by-step procedure. • Solve a puzzle or problem. • Answer questions on the topic. • Adapt the information for a practical experience.	• Create a simulation, example, or demonstration. • Write an interview for a story character. • Role-play a character or a scene. • Write a play about the reading. • Act out the meaning of vocabulary words or concepts.	• Use a manipulative. • Design an experiment. • Follow an assembly line. • Play a game. • Create an exhibit. • Work in a center. • Create a puppet show. • Build a replica. • Make cutouts of people and places to record facts.	• Listen to a tape, CD, or recording. • Study video clips. • Read with a partner. • Write and share with a partner. • Participate in a discussion of the text. • Create a literary circle for related reading. • View a reenactment.

Figure 4.10	Reading Stations and Centers			
Reading Stations	*Writing Stations*	*Manipulative Stations*	*Conversation Stations*	*Comprehension Stations*
• Reference • Research • Book nook • Book reviews • Critic centers • Newspaper reviews	• Create a book • Writing response • Author's journal • Reflection • Pen pal postings • Composing • Mailbox • Poetry corner • Foldables • Character diaries	• Scrapbooking • Creative arts • Vocabulary sort • Item tubs • Puzzle place • Folder activities • Assembly line • Book making • Skill games • Stick picks	• Character debuts • Interviews • Learn a word • Vocab gab • Novel study • Listening • Reenactments • Simulations • Games • Stomp romp • Debate duo	• Brain teasers • Graphic organizer • Game show • Sports trivia • Computer lab • Observation log • Put it to a beat • Skills gala • Processing center

Figure 4.11	Color-Coded Folders/Activities	
Green *Growing*	Curriculum rewinding	Filling in a gap indicated by a lack of background knowledge vital to learn the information.
Yellow *Ray of Sunshine*	Grade-level	Practicing on the targeted standard, concept, or skill.
Red *All Fired Up!*	Curriculum fast-forwarding	Challenging at a higher level of thinking, because has proven knowledge of the upcoming information.

Materials for Reading Response Stations

Use a Variety of Paper

Shape	Texture	Size	Color	Design

Use Different Types of Paper

Construction paper	Copy paper	Sentence strips	Poster board
Notebook paper	Stationery	Sticky notes	Adding machine tape
Index cards	Cardboard	Paper bags	Plastic bags
Envelopes	Onion skin	Transparencies	Notepad

Try These Other Tools for Writing

Dry-erase board	Chalkboard	Cloth	Foldables

Use Different Writing Implements

Size:	Short	Long	Chunky	Thin
Type:	Pencils	Pens	Chalk	Colored pencils
	Markers	Highlighters	Crayons	Clipboards with paper

Technology Equipment for Stations

Equipment

MP3 player with earbuds	DVD player	Camera
Overhead projector	Desk computer	Laptop computer
Calculator	Document reader	CD player
Handheld game	Printer	Recorder
Camcorder	SMART Board	Scanner
Fax machine	Walkie-talkie	

Internet Sources and Software

MySpace.com	Class Web site	Web search	Blog
PowerPoint	Word processor	Weather bug	CAD program
Web quest	Chatroom	iComic	iTunes
Print Shop	Excel	Clipart	Kidspiration

Comfortable Additions

For seating: Carpet squares, rocking chair, area rug, chair, sofa, desk
For enjoyment: Lamps, stuffed animals, plants, bookmarks, bottled water, pillows

Topic-Related Resources

Text	Graphs	Directions	Graphics	Pictures
Journals	Time lines	Scrapbook	Logs	Portfolios
Word lists	References	Magazines	Brochures	Skill charts

Cubing

Cubing is a learning strategy that provides opportunities for students to use and share their thinking in relation to a reading standard, topic, character, event, setting, vocabulary word, or main idea. Each side of the cube is labeled with a direction using the information gained from reading the text or related materials. Cubes may be color coded to reflect diverse learning abilities. For example, an orange cube could display six intervention activities for struggling readers, while a blue cube could present six challenging activities for comprehending, fluent readers. Use cubing activities to add novelty to processing information.

Cubing activities build on strengths. If a student has difficulty understanding a skill or concept, incorporate the learner's talents, abilities, or strengths to learn the skill. For example, a student with musical abilities can learn the skill by using it in a song, rap, or poem. Cubing activities can also be designed to address weaknesses. Cubing activities can also be created to be fun, interesting, and stimulating. They are intriguing tools to teach standards, problem solving, and higher-order thinking skills (see Figure 4.12).

Figure 4.12 Cubing Activities

Reading Cube	Thinking Cube
• Explain the plot. • Give the character's attributes. • Draw the setting. • Create an event time line. • Place the facts on a graphic organizer. • Summarize the passage.	• List. • Describe. • Argue. • Apply. • Conclude. • Evaluate.
Visual/Spatial Cube	Bodily/Kinesthetic Cube
• Design a poster. • Create a graphic organizer. • Color code. • Make a collage. • Create a banner. • Design an ad.	• Create a motion to teach a fact. • Role-play. • Demonstrate with objects. • Build a model. • Play charades. • Create cheers with actions.
Multiple Intelligences Cube	After Reading Cube
• Illustrate. • Plot information. • Role-play. • Create a poem. • Take a stand. • Relate it to your world.	• Write a summary. • Create a game. • Use a manipulative. • Create a poster. • Develop a song. • Reflect in a journal.

Various Ways to Identify the Cubing Task Number

- Number the list. Roll the dice to identify the item on the list to complete.
- Write each direction on a small strip of construction paper. Place the strips in a container and ask each student to draw one strip.
- Use a spinner numbered from 1 to 6.
- Have students in the group number off from 1 to 6.
- Have students write down a mystery number from 1 to 6. They reveal and share the selected numbers. If two or more students have the same number, they complete the same assignment independently. The responses will vary.

Suggestions for Designing a Cube

- Apply various levels of questioning as outlined on Bloom's taxonomy. Here are some examples:
  - Find the word that means_____. (Knowledge level)
  - How is this information valuable to our community? (Evaluation level)
- Incorporate learning styles in the reading activities. For example, an activity for the concrete learner could be "Design a model to demonstrate the _____."

On the Flip Side

This activity engages students in creating questions about a reading assignment for the class. Divide the class into three-member teams.

1. Give each team six pieces of paper for the question cards. Use a different shape for each team.

2. Assign a section of the text to each team.

3. Encourage the team to find a comfortable place to read and work.

4. Direct the team to create six important questions with their answers.

5. Write a question on one side of each card.

6. Write the answer on the other side of one of the other questions. Note: The answer must be written on the back of another question.

7. Mix the cards together and distribute them to the class.

8. Students take turns reading the question on the cards.

9. The student with the correct answer says, "Flip side."

10. The student reads the correct answer and the question on the flip side.

11. If the answer is incorrect, repeat the initial question until the correct answer is given.

Variation

Review with the flip side card game. Use the cards later in a center, station, or folder.

Choice

Include student choice in instruction and daily routines whenever doing so is appropriate and feasible. Choice becomes an incentive for learning and creates a sense of ownership. Students can show what they know by using their learning preferences.
Give students opportunities to choose the following:

Seating	Genres	Study buddy
Reading materials	Facts to explore	Interest area
Presentation style	Research sources	Writing implements
Paper type	Study aids	Web resources
Reference materials	Job role or task	Being alone or with others

Use choice boards with the reading models to offer flexible learning strategies. For example, the teacher may ask the reader to select one or more activities from the board. Students usually appreciate opportunities to play a major role in task decisions.

Remember to design the board activities to teach or reinforce content information and meet readers' needs. Figure 4.13 shows an example of a choice board.

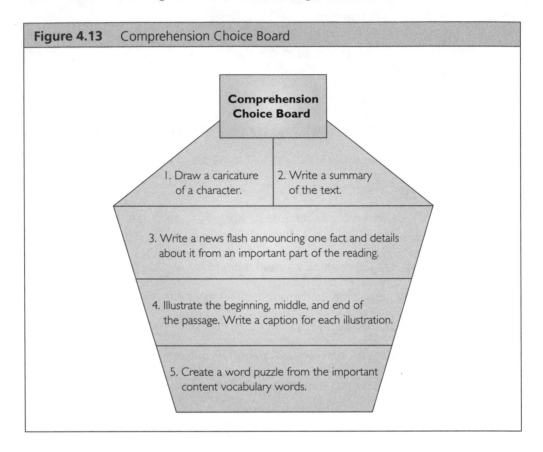

Figure 4.13   Comprehension Choice Board

Comprehension Choice Board

1. Draw a caricature of a character.

2. Write a summary of the text.

3. Write a news flash announcing one fact and details about it from an important part of the reading.

4. Illustrate the beginning, middle, and end of the passage. Write a caption for each illustration.

5. Create a word puzzle from the important content vocabulary words.

SUMMARY

The models of reading detailed in this chapter are instructional planning tools. After collecting assessment data, select the most appropriate model to coordinate the reader's needs with content standards and learning objectives. Adapt the model to customize activities for learners at all knowledge levels related to the standard.

Implement the differentiated instructional strategies to enhance the reading models. Interweave novel activities, such as agendas, cubing, and choice boards, in planning. Strategically select the model and strategies to differentiate instruction as you chart the course for each individual's reading journey.

VOCABULARY 5

Better Than Money in the Bank

In rhymes, menus, movies,

And raps, you will see them there.

When you learn new vocabulary words,

You can use them easily everywhere.

When you master a new word,

And use it with ease in the right place,

It is stored in your vocabulary bank,

Until you say or write it in the right space.

Vocabulary words can make

Others think you are very, very smart.

You can use them in important speeches,

Or write one to touch good friend's heart.

—Chapman and King

VOCABULARY IS A KEY COMPONENT OF READING FLUENCY AND comprehension in every subject. This chapter is designed to give educators tools and strategies for providing vocabulary learning opportunities that meet the diverse needs of all learners in the differentiated classroom.

IDENTIFYING AND SELECTING VOCABULARY WORDS

Commercially made reading programs and subject area textbooks present a vocabulary list for each lesson. The teacher needs to use the identified words as a resource.

Strategically identify words from the list and content that are appropriate for the students. The preassessment data and the teacher's judgment guide this process.

After words are selected, the teacher decides which words to chunk, or group, together to create the most effective learning experiences. Choose the number of words students can understand, retain in memory, and apply. Too often, teachers use long, published lists for instruction and then wonder why the students can't remember all the words. They experience cognitive overload.

As a word is introduced, it goes into short-term memory. If the word is not used, it is quickly forgotten. It needs to be processed and applied in meaningful ways to move into long-term memory. Avoid teaching a word in isolation. Remind students to connect the word with prior experience and knowledge and make new connections in their own worlds to master the word and take ownership of it.

The terms *sight vocabulary* and *sight words* are easily confused.

- *Sight vocabulary* includes all the words an individual recognizes without effort. To build sight vocabulary, rehearse the pronunciation and meaning of the word in different ways until the reader uses it automatically. Students know a word when it becomes a part of their social language and inner speech, or self-talk.

- *Sight words* do not conform to our common pronunciation guides. They "do not play by the rules." For example, words such as *of, to,* and *you* are sight words (Gipe, 2002).

PREASSESSING VOCABULARY WORDS

Preassess to identify words on the vocabulary list that the students already know. Analyze the results, strategically plan, and teach the unknown words to an individual, small group, or total class.

Preassessment 1: Color My World

Use Color My World as an assessment tool to identify words the student has mastered and to create a list of words the student does not know. Provide the student with sticky tabs, highlighters, crayons, colored dots, or pencils in varying colors. This activity is an ideal assessment for identifying each student's knowledge of the words and obtaining immediate results. The reader marks new vocabulary words using these directions:

Green	(Go)	I know this word and use it with ease.
Yellow	(Caution)	I know a little about this word.
Red	(Stop)	I do not know this word.

Teach each student to use this strategy to label words in text, lists, notes, and fact sheets. This strategy shows the student the value of using self-monitoring with vocabulary words.

Preassessment 2: Meet and Greet!

Meet and Greet is an activity that identifies words that need more work for mastery. It gives each student a sense of responsibility, as personal knowledge of each word is analyzed.

- Post a word list from a new study.
- Have students fold a sheet of paper into a "burrito" or tri-fold.
- Ask students to write the headings shown in Figure 5.1 as titles for each section of their papers.
- Place each vocabulary word in the appropriate column.

Figure 5.1 Meet and Greet New Words		
Words I Know	Words I Have Seen or Heard but Do Not Use	Words I Have Never Seen or Heard

Preassessment 3: Mystery Word

This activity builds anticipation, curiosity, and excitement for learning a new word. Use the strategy several days before the unit begins to entice learners to investigate and discover new words.

1. Choose an unknown, key word from the topic.

2. Post the word using large, visually attractive letters.

3. Use these questions to stimulate thinking in relation to the mystery word.
    - What will we learn about this new word?
    - Why is this word used?
    - How will the new word fit into our new unit of study?

Variation 1

Choose a key word from an upcoming unit one week before the introduction of the word. Add one letter of the word to the posting each day and challenge students to guess the word. Provide a blank space for each letter in the word.

Variation 2

Post an unfamiliar key word from a unit of study. write a new clue each day and have the students guess the word's meaning.

Variation 3

Write the key word from the unit of focus on a large card.

For example, the key word is *fraction.* Students write each fact they know about the term on an individual sticky note. They brainstorm more words or phrases related to the term. Write the responses under or beside the word to create a "visual associations" list, or definition for each word. This activity can be used as a preassessment tool to identify the students' prior knowledge related to the word.

Here are examples of prior knowledge students might show regarding various key words:

Fractions:	proper	improper	numerator	denominator
Greece:	gods	goddesses	ruins	Parthenon
Topography:	isthmus	prairie	mountain	peninsula

LEARNING NEW WORDS

An effective way to reach individual learners is to relate each new vocabulary word to the students' background knowledge and experiences. Use strategies and activities to make connections between the content material and the learners' worlds.

The mind is intrigued with mysteries, challenges, and discoveries. Treat the introduction of a vocabulary word as an adventure by creating anticipation and excitement. This phase of learning is important because the desire to learn a new word is easily turned on or off during this stage of the lesson. Select words wisely. Maintain the reader's interest with a variety of novel strategies that focus attention on the word.

Vocabulary words are selected from the content lesson. The typical way to teach a new word is for the teacher to guide students through a procedure like this:

1. Look at the word.

2. Hear the word.

3. Pronounce the word with the teacher.

4. Spell it.

5. Write it.

6. Look it up in the dictionary, glossary, or text.

7. Write a sentence using the word.

What is wrong with this method? It is not wrong. It is one effective way to introduce a new word to students. However, it is not the only way. If this method is overused, the activity becomes a routine procedure and a mundane, nonthinking task strategy—the vocabulary rut of today's classrooms. Learners in the differentiated reading classroom need to work with many strategies to learn new words.

Using a variety of strategies and activities adds novelty to each learning experience. A good way to start is with ideas from a Learn a Word Choice Board (see Figure 5.2), which guide and intrigue the student to work further with the word. A word could be assigned to each student, or the students could choose a way to teach the word to others from the board. Call on volunteers to share some of their favorite ways to learn a new word with the class.

Figure 5.2   Learn a Word Choice Board

Connect the word with something in the student's world and discuss it.	Locate the word in the text and read the paragraph to get context meaning.	Create a design that depicts the meaning of the word.
Make a mnemonic to remember the word and its meaning.	Make a word puzzle or a game.	Contrast the word with something else.
Write a poem with the word, giving its meaning and related facts. Illustrate it.	Tell a story using the word three times in the plot.	Teach the word and its meaning in a memorable way to a classmate.
Explain how the word is used in the text.	Divide the word into syllables. Chant and tap the syllables.	Create a song, poem, cheer, or rap using the word as the topic.
Role-play the meaning.	Design a banner or flag for the word and its meaning.	Write an ad to sell the word.

Variation

When students are able to find the chosen word in several places in the text, create partners or small groups to share the word, its meaning(s), and various ways it is used in each location.

Vocabulary as Vocabulary

Demystify the word *vocabulary* by introducing it. Give students a simple definition of the word *vocabulary,* such as "a word that is read or said and used easily in the right place." For example, write the word *vocabulary* with the word *vocal* directly below it. Underline the first four letters in each word to illustrate that the base word means "voice." Discuss the many meanings of the term until students can use it in lessons and activities. Read the poem that introduces this chapter.

Word Discovery

Use a discovery method to add novelty to a vocabulary lesson. For example, introduce a word as a mystery. This strategy helps the reader learn how to use clues to discover word meanings. Write the word on the board; have the class pronounce it. Use these directions to challenge the class:

1. Post the word.

2. Find the new word in a scavenger hunt in the selected passage.

3. Give a thumbs-up when it is found.

4. Read the word.

5. Read the sentences surrounding the word.

Adjustable Assignments

Each student has a unique knowledge base in relation to each new word. Through experiences, learners build their own repertoires of knowledge related to the topic. In planning differentiated vocabulary learning, an adjustable assignments model can be adapted to any subject or grade level across the curriculum (Chapman & King, 2008).

Figure 5.3 shows the knowledge base levels of a group of students introduced to a set of vocabulary words for a unit of study. The three columns reflect three levels of mastery. Students who have little or no prior experience with the content words are on the "curriculum rewinding" level. Many students in the class have some knowledge of the word; this group is on grade level. Students who know the word and use it appropriately in reading, writing, and language are working on the "curriculum fast-forwarding level."

Individuals vary in the amount of information they can remember. Select the number of vocabulary words to accommodate the reader's retention ability. After the words are introduced and taught, they need to be practiced and used in varied ways during the lessons until they enter the student's long-term memory. When this occurs, celebrate the learner's ownership of the words.

TWENTY-FIVE WAYS TO TEACH VOCABULARY

A student needs a strong vocabulary to become a fluent reader. The strategies in this section are designed to teach vocabulary skills using key words in the content information. The games and activities are student-friendly and practical. They engage the students' intelligences and learning modalities. Teachers can adapt the differentiated strategies to the lesson content for any subject area to meet the diverse needs of each reader in their classrooms.

1. Senseless Sillies

Students enjoy becoming familiar with words through novel and humorous activities. Here are some challenging, fun ways to learn new words.

- Write silly sentences, stories, or riddles with the word.
- Use the word in rhymes and jingles.
- Connect the vocabulary word and the linking word in a sentence. The sentence may be silly. In fact, students often remember silly sentences best. Challenge students to include the definition. Create a cartoon to illustrate the sentence.
- Write tongue twisters using the new words.

Figure 5.3	Adjustable Assignment for Introducing Vocabulary Words		
	Curriculum Fast-Forwarding	*Grade Level*	*Curriculum Rewinding*
C How do I teach this group?	• Write a story using the word in a different genre. • Read the story to a classmate. • Create a word puzzle with the word. (See "A Word on Words.") • Develop a word game to play with a partner. • Design a word web with related words. • Evaluate the word's value to the topic. Write a sales pitch to sell the word to a publisher for a dictionary.	• Use the word in a skit or cartoon. • Review the word in the glossary, word list, chart, diagram, and text passage. • Illustrate the meaning for a word wall. • Create a memory device for the word. • Reread the passage using a synonym or phrase to replace the word.	• Show pictures with the word's meanings. • Give each word a debut. • Read easy passages that contain the word. • Say each syllable and repeat it several times. • Teach memory tricks and gimmicks for the word. • Act the Word: Say it, give the definition, and do an action to illustrate the meaning. • Plan activities for reader interaction with the word, such as cutting it out, pasting it, and designing it.
B What do they need next?	• Needs praise for knowing the word. • Needs to know how to use and apply the words in varied ways.	• Needs ownership of the word. • Needs a novel way to learn the word. • Needs to be able to analyze context clues.	
A What do they know?	• Reads the word automatically. • Knows the word's meaning. • Uses the word correctly in context.		• Needs an effective introduction of the word to own the word. • Needs to learn word's meaning. • Needs opportunities to adapt the word for personal use.
		• Has some knowledge of the word. • Recognizes the word. • Has no recall of the meaning.	• Has no knowledge of the word. • Has little knowledge of the word.

SOURCE: Adapted from Gregory & Chapman, 2007.

2. Box It!

The Box It strategy (Figures 5.4 and 5.5 on the next page) illustrates the structural parts of a vocabulary word. It provides an opportunity for the learner to use the new word in meaningful ways. A base word (for example, *lock*) stands alone without losing its meaning when a prefix (*un*-lock) or suffix (lock-*ing*) is added. The Box It activity can be used to introduce new words in other ways, as in these examples:

base or root word	prefix	suffix	sentence
definition	illustration	synonym	antonym
slogan	rhyme	word origin	joke

Figure 5.4 Box It Strategy		
Choose a word with a prefix and suffix.		
Write the prefix.	Write the base or root word.	Write the suffix.
Create a design.	Write the definition.	Create a sentence.

Figure 5.5 Box It Example		
Unlocking		
Un	lock	ing
(Design)	Removal of a fastener (Definition)	He is unlocking the door with a golden key. (Sentence)

3. Words in Motion

The Words in Motion activity is an easy, fun way to learn new words. This strategy teaches word meanings using body movement or actions. Look through the vocabulary list and choose a group of words with meanings that lend themselves to a motion. Try this activity (adapted from Chapman & King, 2009) with each word:

1. Look at the word and pronounce it.

2. Say the meaning.

3. Choose a motion to match the meaning.

4. Pronounce the word. Say the meaning with the motion.

5. Repeat the meaning and motion two more times.

4. Vocabulary Beat!

Vocabulary Beat is a strategy that teaches students how to remember words and their meanings by using them with a beat or a rhythm. Discuss musical jingles and rhymes in well-known commercials. Ask students to make up vocabulary versions. Remind students to use a familiar tune. This way the class's concentration will be on the content information rather than the song's tune. Ask the class to join together in a vocabulary performance activity:

1. Divide the class into groups.

2. Assign a new vocabulary word to each group for the word *debut*.

3. Ask each group to create a rap, jingle, chant, poem, or song for the new word.

4. Give students time to present their words in a brief vocabulary performance.

Coin Study

The vocabulary words are *penny, nickel, dime,* and *quarter.* Groups make a verse for the definition of their coin to the song "Are You Sleeping?"

A penny is worth one cent.	*A nickel is worth five cents.*
A penny is worth one cent.	*A nickel is worth five cents.*
A copper coin.	*A round silver coin.*
A copper coin.	*A round silver coin.*
One, two, three, four.	*Five, ten, fifteen, twenty.*
One, two, three, four.	*Five, ten, fifteen, twenty.*
Count your pennies.	*Count your nickels.*
Count your pennies.	*Count your nickels.*
A dime is worth ten cents.	*A quarter is worth twenty-five cents.*
A dime is worth ten cents.	*A quarter is worth twenty-five cents.*
A tiny, silver coin.	*A big silver coin.*
A tiny, silver coin.	*A big silver coin.*
Ten, twenty, thirty, forty.	*Twenty-five, fifty, seventy-five, a dollar.*
Ten, twenty, thirty, forty.	*Twenty-five, fifty, seventy-five, a dollar.*
Count your dimes.	*Count your quarters.*
Count your dimes.	*Count your quarters.*

—Chapman and King

5. Evening Learning Opportunity (ELO)

Evening Learning Opportunities (ELOs) are homework assignments that intrigue learners, interest them, and challenge their minds. They give students opportunities to work with unfamiliar information and build background knowledge.

For example, present the upcoming vocabulary word *metric* one to two weeks before it is introduced in the lesson. Give students a piece of paper with the mystery word *metric.* From the time the assignment is made until the word is taught, challenge students to search for everything they can find related to the word. One rule to state clearly is that "you can ask anyone about the unknown word except me." Students enjoy keeping secrets from the teacher as they discover the word on items in their kitchens, bathrooms, and laundry rooms. They find the word on the Web, in text, and in interviews with adults and with classmates. Examples, definitions, descriptions, and explanations are recorded on the mystery word sheet. Excitement will be evident as the detectives share their discoveries.

6. The Same Game

The Same Game illustrates how one word and other words can have the same meaning. The activity provides an opportunity for the student to make choices and interact with a classmate while learning new words.

1. Choose a word from the vocabulary list with several synonyms; for example, *boulevard*.

2. Write the selected vocabulary word with the meaning on the board or a chart.

3. Tell students to find partners and name each other A and B

4. Partner A uses the chosen word in a sentence; for example, "I walked down the *boulevard*."

5. Partner B repeats the sentence and replaces the vocabulary word with a synonym; for example, "I walked down the *street*."

6. Partner A uses another synonym in the same sentence.

7. The game continues until students have used several examples.

8. Call on partner teams to give the synonyms and use them to make a class list under the key word.

9. Examine each item on the brainstormed list and write an *S* beside the words that are synonyms; for example, *boulevard*: *street, road, avenue, thoroughfare*.

7. The Match Game

Make a deck of synonym cards for the Match Game. Place each word on a separate card from the A and B list as in this example:

A	B
figure	calculate
round	spherical

Divide the class in half and label the teams A and B. Give each student on the A team one word from list A. Give each student on the B team one word from list B. Ask students to follow these steps:

1. Use the word on your card to create a sentence. Write the sentence on a strip of paper.

2. Take the word with the sentence and find the classmate who has your synonym's partner.

3. Read your sentence with the identified synonym to your partner.

4. Read the sentence again, substituting your partner's synonym for your word.

5. Repeat Steps 3 and 4 with partner B reading his or her sentence.

NOTE: Collect the synonyms and sentences to create an exciting game for a matching and sorting synonym station.

Variation

Play the game with antonyms, homonyms, words and definitions, math symbols and their meanings, or a word with an illustration.

8. Artful Antics

Antonyms are words that have opposite meanings. Illustrate each word in an antonym pair with cartoons. Here are some sample antonym pairs:

courageous/cowardly	scarce/plentiful	old/new
beginning/conclusion	rough/smooth	pain/pleasure
harmful/safe	domestic/foreign	hollow/solid
acquaintance/stranger	amateur/professional	agree/oppose

Variation

1. Play charades with two students acting out the meaning of each word in the antonym pair.

2. Ask the audience to guess the antonym pair.

9. Compound Word Wizard

A compound word is the combination of two base words to form one word. The Compound Word Wizard activity demonstrates the meaning of each word in the compound word.

1. Locate the compound word(s) in the vocabulary list. Examples: *playground, pocketbook,* and *moonlight.*

2. Separate each word into two parts choosing one of these methods:
   - Use a different color to write each part.
   - Highlight each part differently.
   - Box each word in the compound word.
   - Cut the words apart.

3. Illustrate the meaning of the compound word.

10. It Takes Two

Think of compound words beginning with the same first word. Add to these lists:

sun:	sunlight	sunglasses	sunflower	_____
head:	headrest	headset	headstrong	_____
fire:	firefly	firehouse	firefighter	_____
air:	airplane	airport	airline	_____
door:	doorway	doormat	doorstop	_____
out:	outlook	outside	outdated	_____
side:	sideswipe	sidestep	sidekick	_____

11. Analogy Action

An analogy shows the reader how words are alike or different. Analogies provide relationships or associations between words and create meaning for the learner by making words easier to remember.

1. Give several sample analogies; for example, *Train* is to *track* as *car* is to *road*.

2. Check to make sure the same word or phrase can be used interchangeably in each analogy pair; for example, " . . . travels on a. . . ." becomes "A train travels on a track," and "A car travels on a road."

To work through some examples, complete the word relationships in these analogies:

1. _____: messy :: young : old ["is the opposite of"] Choices: organized, aged, brave

2. arctic : cold :: tropics : _____ ["feels"] Choices: hot, south, desert

3. reptile : _____ :: mammal : hairs ["is covered with"] Choices: gills, scales, skin

NOTE: Remind students to identify the relationship of the given word pair.

12. Share and Compare

1. Form cooperative groups of three or four students.

2. Name a key word or term from the unit of study; for example, *rain forest, addition, Paul Bunyan.*

3. Fold a large piece of newsprint into two equal sections. Label the sections A and B.

4. Instruct students to place this sentence with blanks in section A: The [word, phrase, or topic] is like [phrase or noun] because [tell how they are alike]. Here are some examples:

   • The rain forest is like an umbrella because it creates a cover over the ground.
   • A trapezoid is like a rectangle because it has four sides.

5. In the B section, illustrate the comparisons and label the words' common attributes.

Variation

Explore contrasting attributes for the key word using this sentence:

_____ is not like a _____ because _____.

13. Trio Masterpiece

Choose vocabulary words from the unit of focus whose meanings can be illustrated. Form groups of three and give each group three large, blank index cards.

1. One student writes the vocabulary word with the diacritical markings and part of speech underneath the word.

2. The second student writes the word's meaning on the card.

3. The third student illustrates the word's meaning on the card.

4. The group places the same symbol on the back of each card in their sets. Examples include star, pound symbol, happy face, asterisk.

5. Students pass the completed cards to the teacher.

6. The cards are shuffled and dealt to everyone

7. Each student goes on a search to find the matches for the word, definition, or illustration.

8. The trio creates a clever presentation for the class to teach the word.

9. Display the words, definitions, and illustrations or Trio Masterpieces by creating a vocabulary gallery.

Variation

Place the cards on the backs of students to create a matching game.

14. Crisscross Challenge

The Crisscross Challenge activity teaches students how to cross-reference vocabulary words. Try this strategy after the introduction of glossaries and other reference resources:

1. Have students find partners.

2. Post a vocabulary word from the text lesson.

3. Challenge partners to find the word in the chapter, unit, glossary, or index.

4. When the team has cross-referenced the word, one student places a finger on the word in the text, while the partner points to the word in the reference.

5. When partners find the word in both places, they shout "Crisscross!" together.

6. Each partner writes the word on the front of an index card with the definition on the back.

7. Call on partners to read the information they find.

8. Score the crisscross success by counting the number of completed cards.

NOTE: The cards can be used as flashcards to review the vocabulary words.

15. T-Toon

A T-Toon is a cartoon design on a T-shirt. Ask the students to bring a plain T-shirt from home. The designs can be created on a large piece of paper cut in the shape of a T-shirt.

1. Make a list of vocabulary words whose meanings can be illustrated.

2. Each student chooses a favorite word from the list.

3. Have the students draw a cartoon illustrating the word and its meaning on the shirt. For example, these vocabulary words and definitions are from a transportation unit.
   - *Vehicle:* Draw a picture of any means of transportation.
   - *Transport:* Draw a picture of a vehicle carrying passengers or things.
   - *Passenger:* Draw people or animals in a vehicle with a driver.

4. Write the key word in a jingle, advertisement, or poem on the back of the T-shirts.

5. Place synonyms in a "graffiti way" on the T-shirts.

6. Schedule a day for the students to present, wear, or display the T-Toons.

7. Display the T-Toons on a clothesline or coat hangers.

16. Cartoon Capers

1. Create a cartoon related to the topic using vocabulary words.

2. Write dialogue in appropriate speech bubbles.

3. Highlight or use some other distinguishing marking to identify each vocabulary word in the cartoon.

Variation

Use a cartoon strip with each section representing a sequence and procedure. Each frame of the comic strip needs to have at least one vocabulary word included in the speech bubble dialogue.

17. Multiple Madness

Challenge students to create sentences using multiple meanings of the same word. Include various forms of the word. Here are some examples.

fly: Does a <u>fly fly</u> faster when it <u>flies</u> in an airplane?

bark: The grouchy man <u>barked</u>, "Go away" when the dog <u>barked</u> at the tree <u>bark</u>.

walk: Did you <u>walk</u> on the <u>walk</u> when he said, "Take a <u>walk</u>!"?

18. Words on Word

Play this game in a center or station, with a small group, or as an independent assignment to practice using vocabulary words and their definitions.

1. Choose an important word from the content vocabulary list.

2. Write each letter of the key word on a separate piece of paper.

3. Arrange the letters of the word vertically on the floor.

4. Choose additional vocabulary words with at least one letter in common with each letter in the key word.

5. Write a definition clue for each word.

6. Challenge another team to solve the Word on Words puzzle. Here's an example, with the key word being *skeleton*.

a.	s _ _ _ _	Supports the upper body
b.	_ k _ _ _	Protection for the brain
c.	_ _ _ e _ _ _	Another name for the kneecap
d.	_ l _ _	A large bone in the upper arm
e.	_ _ _ _ e	The bone that causes the foot to rotate
f.	t _ _ _ _	A large bone in the lower leg
g.	_ o _ _ _	A place where two bones connect
h.	_ _ _ _ _ n _ _ _	A name for fingers and toes

Answer Key

| a. spine | b. skull | c. patella | d. ulna |
| e. ankle | f. tibia | g. joint | h. phalanges |

Here's another example: the key word is *train*.

a.	_ t _ _	Cars _____ at the railroad crossing.
b.	r _ _	The caboose is usually _____.
c.	_ _ a _ _	The wheels of the train roll on the _____.
d.	_ _ _ i _ _	The first car on a train is the _____.
e.	_ _ n _ _ _ _ _	The _____ is the person in charge of the train.

Answer Key

| a. stop | b. red | c. track | d. engine | e. conductor |

19. Five Up

Students in small groups prepare five large cards, each with a vocabulary word on one side and the word's meaning and/or illustration on the back of the card.

1. Place the cards in a stack.

2. Call on five students to come to the front of the room.

3. The five students each draw one vocabulary card and form a line in front of the room.

4. Each student turns over the chosen card so the class sees the definitions.

5. The class silently reads the definitions on the five cards.

6. Students at their seats place their heads on their desks and close their eyes.

7. Each student holding a card gently taps one seated student.

8. When the five students have tapped someone and returned to the front of the room, they say, "Five up!"

9. Students take turns guessing who tapped them. If the first student correctly responds with the name of the person who tapped him, that student must read the definition for the vocabulary word and guess the word.

10. If the student answers correctly, he draws a vocabulary card and takes the place of the person who tapped him. If he guesses the word incorrectly, the student holding the card stays with the Five Up group for the next round of the game.

11. Continue the game until all vocabulary words are guessed.

20. Stick Picks

Write each mastered vocabulary word on one side of an ice cream stick, tongue depressor, or paint stirrer. On the other side of the stick, write the meaning and antonym, homonym, or sentence with the word. Place the Stick Picks in a small, decorated can or box. Store the sticks in categories, using rubber bands or placing them in envelopes for easy access. Here are some ways to use the Stick Picks to categorize the mastered words:

- Alphabetically
- Common attributes
- Topic
- Subject area
- Syllables

21. Know Cans

The student personalizes a can by covering it with words or hobbies that reflect special interests. The student writes the mastered new vocabulary word on a slip of paper and places it in the Know Can. The word collections can be used periodically for "canned" reviews.

22. Stomp Romp

Place new words on shoe outlines or footprints. Create a path of vocabulary words around the room, in the hallway, or on the playground. The student strolls down the vocabulary path, stopping and stomping beside each word and pronouncing it.

Variation 1

Tell students to time their vocabulary journeys. Plot the time. Challenge the readers to increase their speed on each trip down the path.

Variation 2

Partners stand on each side of the first word. They stroll side by side as they create a beat while saying each word.

23. Word Game Trivia

Students enjoy using topic vocabulary and trivia in popular games. Adapt these learning activities for one student, a team, or a class using a game format such as one of these:

Crosswords	Riddles	Rhymes	Concentration
Jeopardy	Wheel of Fortune	Survivor Challenges	Password
Bingo	Hangman	Card Games	Charades
Pictionary	Lingo	Who Wants to Be a Millionaire?	

24. Vocabulary Sketch

Draw the outline or shape of an important object, country, person, or symbol in the study. Students write the vocabulary words, definitions, synonyms, antonyms, or attributes on the shape outline.

Variation

Create a Vocabulary Sketch mystery activity. Students draw an outline of an important person in a study or a character in a book and create an outline of the individual. Tell them to write related vocabulary words and attributes around the outline. Have students exchange the sketches so classmates can read the clues and guess the name of the character. Display the Vocabulary Sketches with the character's name written in large letters on the character.

25. Curiosity Collection Corner

Designate an area for students to post favorite or most difficult vocabulary words to learn. Challenge them to find words that raise curiosity or pose a challenge. Create a list of the words students or a group want to learn. Include words found during and after school. Here are some possible sources of words:

Newspapers	Malls	Internet sites	Books	Advertisements
Videos	Labels	Sporting events	Movies	Menus
Packages	Magazines	Hallways	Textbooks	Neighborhood signs
Television programs			Computer programs	

Vocabulary Visuals

Create vocabulary visuals, or word displays, in various ways to grab students' attention and maintain high interest in using the display as a reference. Form each word in a unique way and post it in a visible place or space while introducing it. Use an outline of an object in the unit of study and ask students to write the word on the shape. Creating a shape helps students mentally link information to the content. Often the selected shape depicts the meaning of the word, category, or topic. Direct learners to add designs or features to shapes to make them novel.

Use vocabulary visuals during a unit of study, as a bridge from one topic to another, or to review key words. Classroom locations for visuals include

Backs of bookcases	Ceiling	Mobiles
Blinds	Chart stands	Walls
Borders	Clotheslines	Window
Bulletin boards	Curtains	Window shades
Cabinet doors	Desks (front/sides)	

The word wall is a popular way to display word lists. Each new word is displayed as it is introduced. Below, various word wall designs are described with more ideas for creating vocabulary visuals. Suggested activities are included.

Door Magic

1. Obtain a discarded refrigerator or vehicle door and mount it on the wall. Students enjoy these distinctive display items.

2. Paint or tape a decorative frame border around the door.

3. Use magnetic or colorful letters to display illustrated vocabulary words.

Base Word Wall

1. Create three columns on a bulletin board, chart, poster, or wall space.

2. Label the columns "Prefix," "Base or Root Word," and "Suffix."

3. Provide paper strips, scissors, and markers in an accessible area near the Base Word Wall.

4. Challenge students to add words to the wall.
   - Write the words in a colorful, graffiti way on a paper strip.
   - Cut the word into parts: prefix, root word, and suffix.
   - Write the base word in larger letters and in a unique font.

5. Challenge students to add words to the Base Word Wall when new words are encountered in reading.

Word Substitution Wall

1. Create a chart with four columns.

2. Label the columns "Key Word," "Synonym," "Synonym," and "Synonym."

3. Write a vocabulary word in the key word column and a synonym in the first substitute column.

4. Leave the next synonym column blank until the reader encounters another synonym.

5. Challenge students to add words to the synonym columns as words are encountered in their reading.

Ribbon Wall

1. Hang bright, decorative ribbon from the ceiling or a hook on the wall.

2. Call on a student to staple each new word on the ribbon.

3. Connect the ribbons in creative designs.

Vocabulary Vine

Make a Vocabulary Vine to display around a bulletin board, ceiling, or door. Write key words of a topic or unit of study on leaves to attach to the vine. Call on students to add to the vine each time you introduce a vocabulary word.

Borders

Write vocabulary words with bright colors in distinctive ways as special borders on bulletin boards, doorways, desks, bookcases, windows, or work areas.

Design Signs

Create a graffiti board. The learner writes the vocabulary word in a graffiti way and posts it on the board. Encourage the reader to use color, various media, glitter, and dots. Provide paper in various textures, sizes, and shapes. The creative presentation of the word makes it easier to remember. The student signs the designed vocabulary word.

Collection Bank

Create a personalized Word Collection Bank by alphabetizing or categorizing vocabulary words so they are easy to find and use. Create individual, personalized word banks of mastered words using one of these tools:

Index card file	Bookmark
Adding machine tape	Three-ring binder
Inside of a folder	Chain links
Box or lid	Border for individual note-taking pads
Journal	Student-made dictionary

Give Yourself a Hand

Explain that the phrase "Give someone a hand," means to applaud someone. This activity provides a way for students to "give themselves a hand" for each vocabulary success.

Students write a vocabulary word on outlines of their hands each time they discover or learn a new word. This is a form of affirmation or self-praise. Connect the hands of each students with a string or ribbon. Challenge each student to see how many hands are accumulated before the end of the unit or topic of study. The hands created by individual students can be joined for a total-class celebration.

Critter Crawl

Place content words on a critter that fits the topic theme. Display it from wall to wall, creeping around the work area, a door facing, or bulletin board.

CUES TO CONTEXT CLUES

The word *context* means "with words." Context clues are words and phrases in a sentence that provide the meaning of an unknown word. The learner's reading level determines the ability to use context clues. When a passage contains vocabulary words above the student's instructional level, it is difficult to comprehend the text and unlock a word's meaning. Students need to know how to apply context clues automatically.

Identifying Context Clues

The following clues in a text passage often give a description, an informal meaning, or a definition for the unknown word.

Clue 1. Definition in the Text: Word Meaning

Examples:

Precipitation, a form of rain or snow, may keep us from playing outside.

His *determination*, or strong desire to complete his work, helped him reach his goals.

Clue 2. Synonyms: Words That Have the Same Meaning

Examples:

The *enormous* elephant is so *large*, it cannot come through our door.

The *minuscule* critter is so *tiny*, it is viewed with a magnifying glass.

Clue 3. Antonyms: Words That Are Opposites

Examples:

The rabbit was *fast*, but the *slow* turtle won the race.

Billy's mom complained about his *messy* room, so the next day it was *immaculate*.

Clue 4. Examples in Text

Examples:

As the *fruit* is picked, the baskets fill with *oranges*, *apples*, and *pears*.

The fishermen caught many *fish*, including *bream*, *catfish*, and *bass*.

Strategies for Context Clues

Uncover the Unknown

Teach the reader to use these strategies to identify a word in context:

1. Read the entire sentence without the unknown word.

2. Read the sentences or words before and after the unknown word.

3. Look around the word to see if you can find a synonym, an antonym, or examples in the passage.

4. Remove the prefix and/or suffix, then read the base or root word.

5. Find the word's meaning in the dictionary or glossary.

6. Ask a friend.

7. When everything else fails, ask the teacher.

SUBJECT TERMINOLOGY

Each content area has key words the reader needs to know and understand. Many of those words require students to use higher-order thinking. Post key vocabulary words in enticing fonts, colors, and textures in classrooms and throughout the school. It is important teach and showcase terms used in directions when making written and oral assignments. The ability to use and understand these terms is vital for success on assignments and tests in each subject area (Marzano, 2004).

Do not assume a student knows the subject's vocabulary words just because the words were introduced in previous lessons. It is common for a learner to recall a word and know how to pronounce it but lack the understanding to apply the word in the new context. As subject-related terms are encountered, add them to the displayed checklist that students are expected to master. Here is a sample list of math terms commonly found in directions that readers need to know:

add	describe	list	replace
answer	develop	locate	report
calculate	devise	maintain	review
change	diagram	mark	round
check	divide	match	select
choose	do	measure	sequence
classify	draw	multiply	show
compare	estimate	name	simplify
complete	explain	note	solve
compose	figure	plan	subtract
compute	find	practice	support
conduct	formulate	predict	teach

construct	graph	prepare	tell
contrast	group	prescribe	think
copy	hypothesize	rank	trace
create	identify	rationalize	use
debate	illustrate	read	work
define	line up	regroup	write

OVERCOMING MISCUES

A miscue is an oral response that occurs when the reader makes an effort to say a word but the pronunciation is not correct. The reading error may be the result of a phonics error, inadequate sight word recognition skills, or a guess based on incorrect use of context clues. One of the easiest ways to teach students to overcome miscues is to have them search in the passage for words and phrases that are clues to the unknown word.

These guidelines to identify miscues are adapted from the work of Yetta Goodman (1998):

1. Make the reader physically and emotionally comfortable.

2. Sit beside the reader with a copy of the passage.

3. Explain the purposes for identifying miscues.

4. Tell the student to read as though reading to himself or herself.

5. Model various ways to guess the pronunciation of a word.

6. Ask the reader if he or she has any questions.

7. Mark each miscue on the passage copy.

8. Remind the student to guess after 30 seconds elapses.

9. Commend the reader.

Miscue Analysis

The purpose of miscue analysis is to determine the type of mistake the reader is making while attempting to say a word. Make a note of the strategy used when the unknown word is encountered. Does the student use phonics to unlock initial, medial, and final consonant sounds in syllables? Is the student using phonics to unlock the vowel sounds? Make notes of the observed errors with the date. Analyze the types of errors and look for patterns to plan strategies for correcting them. Figure 5.6 can be used when reading for miscue analysis (Clay, 1993).

Figure 5.6   Miscue Analysis Checklist

I. Phrasing and Fluency

A. Reads: _____ Word by word   _____ In short phrases   _____ In longer phrases
                   _____ Uses punctuation

B. Intonation: _____ Emerging   _____ Developing   _____ Effective

C. Reading Rate: _____ Slow   _____ Inconsistent   _____ Adequate
                   _____ Too fast   _____ Adjusted appropriately

II. Troubleshooting

A. Problems solved by: _____ Picture cues   _____ Rereading   _____ Letter sounds
                         _____ Symbols   _____ Pausing

B. Appeals for help: _____ Often   _____ Sometimes   _____ Rarely
                         _____ Not at all

C. Number of words given by the teacher: _____

III. Analysis of Errors

A. Self-corrected miscues that
   _____ did not make sense.
   _____ did not sound right.
   _____ did not look right.

B. Miscues interfered with meaning: _____ Yes   _____ Sometimes   _____ No

IV. Initial Retelling

A. When asked to "tell the passage in your own words," identified the following:
   _____ Main idea   _____ Character   _____ Setting   _____ Important details
   _____ Vocabulary or phrases from reading   _____ Events in sequence
   _____ Events out of sequence   _____ Ending

B. When asked to "tell me more," information was added related to the following:
   _____ Character   _____ Events   _____ Settings   _____ Detail   _____ Endings

V. Follow-Up Questions

A. Did you like what you read?   _____ Yes   _____ No
   Why? Why not? _____

B. What does this story make you think of? _____

What to Do With a Miscue

The miscues below have several possible solutions. Each activity engages the reader. Use the students' favorite "ways of learning" to teach them how to correct their mistakes while reading content information. See examples that follow.

Letter Sound Recognition Errors

- Write the letters in sand, pudding, shaving cream, or lotion.
- Use shoestrings to match uppercase letters and lowercase letters.
- Create the letters with pipe cleaners, dough, licorice, and yarn.

- Practice the letters on a magic slate, a gel bag, a blackboard, or a transparency.
- Identify the letters in alphabet cereal, advertisements, and the names of classmates.
- Race to find letters in easy books, newspapers, magazines, and television guides.

Insertions

- Read easy books.
- Play games with familiar phrases and sentences.
- Allow students to read orally with the teacher.
- Record a student's reading and replay it as the learner follows the words.
- Praise readers when they read a sentence without insertions.

Omissions

- Use reminders to slow down and pay attention to individual words.
- Use a penlight or highlighter to underline words as they are read.
- Record students as they read and ask them to follow the words as they listen to their reading being played back.
- Use choral or partner reading.
- Ignore omissions if the text's meaning is not changed and they are not a habit.

Substitutions

- Emphasize the use of initial and final consonant sounds.
- Read easy books.
- Use the Follow the Leader strategy.
- Read with recorded books.
- Praise readers when they complete a passage without substitutions.

Reversals

- Color code the first and last letters in the word, using one color for the first letter and another color for the last letter.
- Color code the right and left side of the desk, using the same colors chosen for the first and last letter in a word.
- Color code left and right hands.
- Use a piece of cardboard, index card, or strip of paper as a guide under each sentence.
- Use a word processing program to practice typing the word.

Repetitions

- Check word attack skills.
- Have the student read the passage silently before reading it orally.
- Encourage the student to develop awareness of the repetition.

- Build sight word skills.
- Arrange for the student to read with books on a CD or on tape.
- Use choral reading.

MASTER MULTIPLE MEANINGS

Be aware of words with specific meanings in the subject that students may confuse with a common use of the words. When learning words in a particular subject, the student naturally relates the meaning to prior knowledge and connotations. For example, the word *root* appears in the study of plants. It may be confusing when the student begins a study of "square roots" in a math class. Consider the tricky or confusing words with multiple meanings in these lists:

Root

The plant's *root* grew beneath the rock.

The square *root* of nine is three.

Our neighbor yelled when she saw the pig *root* in her flower garden.

It may take time to find the *root* of your problem.

NOTE: The words *root* and *route* can be confusing, too.

Line

The teacher drew a *line* under the word.

We stood in *line* for concert tickets.

The fishing *line* broke when she caught a large catfish.

Did you follow the teacher's *line* of thinking?

What is your *line* of work?

Create a time *line* of the music star's life.

Hang the shirt on the clothes*line* to dry.

The first *line* in the story was exciting.

The newspaper head*line* was about the rescue.

A *line* separates the numerator and denominator in a fraction.

The time changed when we crossed the state *line*.

Run

Run the motor of the car to warm the engine on a cold morning.

How many times did Abraham Lincoln *run* for public office?

We watched the cowboys *run* the cattle across the prairie.

Have you watched clear water *run* over rocks in a creek?

Did you *run* up a bill during the long distance call?

His mom asks him to *run* the vacuum cleaner each Saturday.

We need to *run* a set of papers for the next class.

STUDENT MASTERY OF VOCABULARY

A student's mastered vocabulary consists of all of the words in the learner's command. When the learner understands a word's use and knows how to apply it properly, the reader owns the word. A student's mastered vocabulary may include the following:

- The words a person pronounces and uses correctly to communicate through speaking, reading, thinking, and writing
- A word list in alphabetical order
- The words in a language
- The words related to a subject or topic

Mastered Words: Check It Out!

A word is mastered when it is read accurately and automatically. Assess a student's mastered vocabulary by using a word list. There are no context clues or other cue to use when reading from a list; the words are read in isolation. Asking the student to read the words out of context gives an accurate count of words automatically recalled.

Select words from the student's unit of study or a leveled vocabulary list. Use questions, such as those in Figure 5.7, to analyze word mastery.

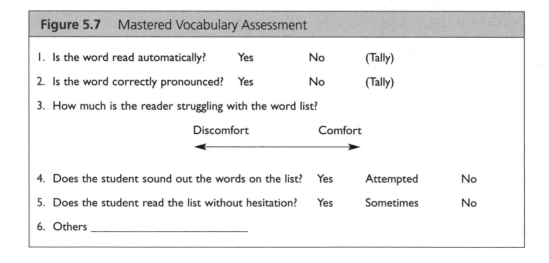

Figure 5.7   Mastered Vocabulary Assessment

1. Is the word read automatically?   Yes   No   (Tally)

2. Is the word correctly pronounced?   Yes   No   (Tally)

3. How much is the reader struggling with the word list?

                          Discomfort   Comfort

4. Does the student sound out the words on the list?   Yes   Attempted   No

5. Does the student read the list without hesitation?   Yes   Sometimes   No

6. Others _____

Teacher-Made Vocabulary Checklists

Create a teacher-made vocabulary checklist. Use essential vocabulary words from topics in the content area. Include words needed for the reader's success. This checklist is an effective tool to assess the reader's word knowledge base before, during, and after the learning.

Summary

Introduce new vocabulary words related to the current topic of study. It is not easy for a student to remember words in isolation, so create meaningful connections. Mnemonic devices and novelty place words in long-term memory, so model gimmicks and tricks students can use to remember words. Show readers how to create and use mnemonics and innovative strategies. Orchestrate experiences with each new vocabulary word using stimulating, unique, and meaningful activities, so the learner's mind takes ownership of the word.

Give readers various ways to learn and remember new words in all subjects. Vocabulary words may be general, or they may be content-specific, technical terms, but connect them to the learner's world and make them personally relevant. Strategically plan differentiated vocabulary instruction with lessons and assignments so each student's quests to learn new words become intriguing challenges.

THE ART OF DECODING **6**

DECODING IS AN ESSENTIAL SKILL READERS USE TO UNDERSTAND unknown words. Decoding a word includes dividing the word into syllables, applying the rules of phonics, and identifying the root or base word. The art of applyings decoding skills lets the reader combine the articulate bits to produce the word's sounds. Most students need to know these skills to become fluent readers. Students encounter words that follow the decoding rules, and with some exceptions, in their vocabulary lessons and reading assignments in all subject areas. Teachers need to infuse the strategies, skills, and rules related to decoding into content lessons.

When a student does not have the background knowledge to apply the rules of phonics, plan systematic, explicit phonics instruction and decoding skills. Integrate the needed rule and skill across the curriculum so the student sees how to apply it in various reading experiences. For example, if the student needs to learn how to apply the controlling *r* rule, use it in a science lesson with the word *equator* and in a math lesson with the word *numerator*.

PHONICS INSTRUCTION

Phonics skill instruction provides a foundation for the student to recognize and pronounce letter sounds and their combinations in print. Students who master letter-sound correspondence have a tool they can use as needed to read more accurately and fluently. Some students struggle to decode words because they have little knowledge or understanding of letter-sound relationships. The application of phonics rules guides readers of all ages to recognize and pronounce words.

Phonics instruction usually receives more emphasis in lower grades than in upper grades, but phonics instruction benefits students in the upper grades who did not develop phonetic awareness in the early grades (National Reading Panel, 2000). Also, some students may simply need a phonics review. Some need to develop their knowledge of letter sounds. Many learners know the rules but cannot apply them automatically as they encounter unknown words. It is essential for readers to know and be able to apply word attack skills.

The art of decoding may be the missing link a student needs to become a successful reader. Innovative, varied, engaging activities give a reader of any age strategies for remembering and applying the rules.

THE PHONICS DOZEN (THE FONIX DUZEN!)

The following section describes a dozen phonics skills a reader should know and be able to apply. Use the activities to teach these important skills with vocabulary development and reading experiences.

Remember, a learner's speaking vocabulary is usually much larger than the reading vocabulary. Students need to sound out a word to hear it and stimulate memories of past associations and experiences with it. The mental images create connections and give meaning to the word.

Actively engage the student in learning phonics rules and generalizations to pronounce words. If the reader knows how to divide words into syllables, the letter sounds in each syllable, and the exceptions to the phonics rules, most words can be decoded and pronounced. Identify key words and examples in the subject's vocabulary words to use with these strategies. Add to the suggestions. Use the step sequence presented here in the Phonics Dozen as needed to teach the readers new ways to remember and apply the skills and rules.

Skill 1: Understand Letters Are Symbols for Sounds That Form Words

Phonics is our alphabet's language. Each letter has one or more distinct sounds. Often two or three letters combine to create blends, digraphs, or diphthongs. The letters take their special places within an arrangement to form words. The reader uses letter sounds to pronounce and recognize words.

When using phonics skills effectively, the student is able to distinguish or decode the sounds of the letters and then combine them to create words. When a student masters the letter sounds and can blend them smoothly and automatically, the learner has tools to use in reading, writing, and speaking.

Alphabet Animals

Students need strategies for remembering letter sounds. The initial consonant and vowel sounds in the lines of Alphabet Animals provide key words the reader can use to recall letter sounds. Use one line to introduce each sound as needed. Use a chanting rhythm to teach the letter sounds, as shown in this example:

Short *a* says /a/. Short *a* says /a/.

/a/ as in Andy. /a/ as in Andy.

Andy Ant acts anxious. Andy Ant acts anxious.

/a/, /a/, /a/—/a/, /a/, /a/. [repeating the short *a* sound]

Amos Ape ate apricots.	Andy Ant acts anxious.
Bobby Bee buys big bikes.	Cathy Cow catches colds.
Cindy Centipede circles cities.	Dottie Dog digs deep ditches.
Eva Emu eats éclairs.	Ed Elephant edits essays.

Felicia Fish found four fans.
George Giraffe gestures gently.
Irene Ibis ices icicles.
Jeffrey Jaguar juggles jars.
Lucy Lion licks lollipops.
Nancy Newt needs nice news.
Opal Opossum opened oatmeal.
Queenie Quail quits quickly.
Silly Seal sings silly songs.
Uly Unicorn uses unicycles.
Victor Vulture visits Vermont.
X-man x-rays *X*'s.
Zeke Zebra zips zippers.

Goofy Goat gets goggles.
Henry Horse hauls heavy hay.
Inky Inchworm inhales insects.
Kate Kangaroo kisses kings.
Mandy Monkey makes music.
Oscar Ostrich offers options.
Paula Parrot paints purple pigs.
Rosie Rabbit races roosters.
Tony Turtle tells tall tales.
Uncle Ugly unhooks umbrellas.
Willie Wolf wears watches.
Yetta Yak yanks yoyos.

Skill 2: Identify the Consonants

Rule A: The consonants constitute all the letters of the alphabet except the vowels. The vowels are *a, e, i, o, u,* and sometimes *w* and *y.*

Rule B: When the same two consonants are side by side in the same syllable, only one of the two consonant sounds is heard: *hallway, grass, mitt.*

Skill 3: Recognize That Hard and Soft Consonants Make Different Sounds

Rule A: The letter *c* makes a hard and a soft sound.

1. The letter *c* makes the hard /k/ sound before *a, o,* and *u*: *castle, copper, custom.*

2. The letter *c* makes the soft /s/ sound before *e, i,* and *y*: *cell, cider, cycle.*

Try this technique to teach the reader how to distinguish between hard and soft consonant sounds. Tell the student to place two or three fingers on the center of the throat while pronouncing words with the hard sound of *c*—/k/—and feel the vocal cords vibrate. Then have the student pronounce words with the soft sound of *c*—/s/— to realize the vocal cords do not vibrate.

Rule B: The letter *g* makes a hard and a soft sound.

1. The letter *g* makes the hard sound before *a, o,* and *u*: *gangster, gorilla, guppy.*

2. The letter *g* makes the soft sound before *e, i,* and *y*: *genius, gigantic, gym.*

Try the vocal cord test to distinguish between the hard and soft *g* sounds.

Goofy Collage

Give students these directions to master the hard *c* and hard *g* sounds.

1. Divide a sheet of paper in half.

2. Cut out pictures and words with the hard *c* and hard *g* sounds.

3. In a graffiti way, do the following:
    - Paste the words and pictures with the hard *c* sound on the top half of the paper.
    - Paste the words and pictures with the hard *g* sound on the bottom half of the paper.

Variation

Repeat the activity for the soft *c* and *g* sounds.

Use the verses in the poem below to teach the soft sounds of the letters *c* and *g*. Select the verses that match the reader's needs.

Camouflaged Consonants: A Poem

c and g are tricky consonants, you see.
They don't say what you expect them to be.
Some vowels change the way c and g sound.
It depends on the vowel hanging around.

c and g will change the sounds they make.
Three vowels soften the noise they create.
If e, i, or y comes after the c,
c makes the /s/ sound easily.

Listen to soft c's whistle and whisper,
As you say center, cyclone, and cinder.
If e, i, or y comes after g,
g makes the /j/ sound easily.

g makes the soft /j/ sound to trick you and me.

Say giraffe, gelatin, gentle, and genie.

Sounds of C and G Chart

Post the following chart for reference as students work with the *c* and *g* sounds. Use a dark, vibrant color as the background for the hard sounds. Use a soft pastel color as a background for the soft sounds.

	a o u	*e i y*
	Hard Sounds	**Soft Sounds**
c	cat, cold, cut	cease, city, cyclone
g	gap, go, gum	genius, giraffe, gym

Rule C: The letter *s* often makes the sound of /z/ at the end of a syllable: *families, enemies, cookies, please, babies, rose.*

S in Disguise: Activity

1. Brainstorm a list of words in which the letter *s* is in "disguise"—making the /z/ sound.

2. In small groups or with partners, play charades with words that follow this rule.

3. Post a class list of words showing *S* in Disguise.

Skill 4: Recognize Consonant Blends

Rule: Two or more consonants using their sounds together are blends. Each letter sound is heard as the blend is pronounced. Blends occurring at the beginnings of words are initial blends. Blends appearing at the end of words are final blends. Blends are often referred to as consonant clusters.

Consonant Blends

bl	cl	fl	gl	pl	sl	br	cr	
dr	fr	gr	pr	sc	scr	sk	sl	sm
sn	sp	spr	st	str	sw	thr	tr	tw

Final Consonant Blends

ft	nd	st	ld	lk	mp

Blend Friends: A Rhyme

> *If two or three consonants blend their sounds together,*
>
> *You hear the sound of each and every letter.*
>
> *Blends are in words at the beginning, middle, or end.*
>
> *Say spook, plant, publish, skate, sport, and friend.*

Blend Blast: Activity

1. Define *blend alliteration* as words with the same beginning sounds. The sounds are made by two or three initial consonants

2. Scan the content passage to find words beginning with consonant blends.

3. Write the words with the same blends in a group, as in these examples:
   - Fresh frozen fruit freezes freaky friends.
   - Dreaming dragons draw dreadfully.
   - Strange straggling strangers stroll straight streets.

4. Ask the students to use blend lists to create alliterations and illustrate them.

5. Share and celebrate.

6. Design an alliteration bulletin board, mobile, or T-shirt.

Skill 5: Use the Sounds of Consonant Digraphs

Rule: When two consonant letters make one sound, they form a consonant digraph. The following list presents consonant digraphs with their sounds and word examples.

ch	/ch/	chain	champ	chart	cheese
ch	/k/	character	chemical	chorus	chrome
ch	/sh/	chef	chalet	charade	chandelier
gh	/g/	ghetto	ghost	ghastly	ghoul
gh	/f/	cough	enough	laugh	tough
ph	/f/	phase	phone	phonics	elephant
sh	/sh/	shade	fish	shark	shawl
wh		whack	wheat	wheel	whine

Voiced

th	/th/	than	that	the	those

Voiceless

th	/th/	thaw	theater	third	thumb

Consonant Digraphs With Silent Letters

gn	/n/	align	gnarl	gnash	gnaw
kn	/n/	knack	knee	knife	knock
wr	/r/	wrangler	wrap	wrestle	wrist
ck	/k/	chicken	clock	flick	shock
tch	/ch/	batch	catch	latch	match
dge	/j/	badge	dodge	fudge	grudge

Digging Digraphs: An Activity

1. Create sentences from words using the same digraph to form alliterations, as in these examples:
   - Shiny sharks shake shimmering shells.
   - Whimpering whales whine while whistling.

2. Illustrate the alliterations.

Digraph Dash: An Activity

1. Take your text, paper, and pencil and meet with a partner.

2. Set a timer for two or three minutes.

3. Individually dash through the text to find words containing digraphs.

4. Write the word and the page number on a list.

5. Exchange lists and check to see that all words contain digraphs.

6. When the Digraph Dash ends, count the number of words on the two lists.

7. Celebrate with the winning partner team.

8. Repeat the game, reducing the time limit. Increase the number of words on the list in each Digraph Dash.

Skill 6: Recognize Long Vowel Sounds

A long vowel is pronounced as it is heard when the alphabet is stated. Remember, the vowels are *a, e, i, o, u,* and sometimes *w* and *y.*

Long vowel sounds are heard in these words: *play, bead, ice, coat, mule, sky.*

NOTE: The letters *w* and *y* may have double duty because they can act as vowels or consonants. For this reason they are often referred to as semivowels.

Rule A: When a word or syllable has a vowel on the end, the vowel usually has a long sound.

> *If a vowel ends a syllable you see,*
> *The vowel says its alphabet name feeling free.*

Examples: baby, be, tricycle, so, music, sky.

Rule B: When two vowels are together, the first one is usually long, and the second one is silent.

> *Strange things happen when two vowels in a syllable meet.*
> *The first one is usually long; the second one is asleep.*

Examples: raid, beat, goat, dye.

Rule C: When a word or syllable contains two vowels, the first vowel is usually long, and the second vowel is silent.

Use the vowel key in Figure 6.1 as a guide for students to use to recall vowel sounds. Create a key chart or poster using vocabulary words in the topic or an area of interest. The words in Figure 6.1 relate to football.

Figure 6.1 Long Vowel Key for Football				
a	*e*	*i*	*o*	*u*
game	tee	line	go	rule
chain	team	hike	goal	uniform

Skill 7: Apply the Rules for the Final *E*

Rule: If a word or syllable has two vowels, and the second vowel is a final *e*, usually the first vowel is long and the final *e* is silent.

> *When a syllable has a vowel, a consonant, and ends in the letter e,*
> *The first vowel is long; the letter e is as silent as it can be.*

Examples: brave, bone, smile, assume, scheme, style.

Skill 8: Recognize That Short Vowels Make Their Own Unique Sounds

Rule: When there is a vowel at the beginning or middle of a syllable followed by a consonant, the vowel is usually short. The vowels are *a, e, i, o, u,* and sometimes *y* and *w*. Short vowels also include the "schwa" sound, which is pronounced "uh" and is the shortest vowel of them all—for example, the sound of the *u* in *circus*. You hear the short vowel sounds in *bat, bed, mitt, socks,* and *luck*.

Short Vowel Key for Football

a	*e*	*i*	*o*	*u*
pass	end	kick	block	run

Scared Short

> *When a syllable has a vowel between consonants without a vowel friend,*
> *It uses the short sound just to hide and pretend.*
> *Listen as you say tap, kit, hop, fin, fat, cut, sit, and win.*
> *Now say each of the words with a silent e on the end.*

Assessment of Vowel Sounds

Ask students to fill in the grid in Figure 6.2 with a word that is an example of the vowel rule.

Figure 6.2 Vowel Play					
	a	*e*	*i*	*o*	*u*
Long					
Short					
Controlling R					

Skill 9: Know the Sounds of Phonograms

A phonogram begins with a vowel. It is a combination of letters ending a word or syllable. Here are some examples:

ab	ame	eat	er	int	ong	ug	ut
ack	an	eed	ice	ip	ook	ule	ute
ad	and	eel	ick	iss	ool	ull	
ag	ang	eep	id	it	oom	um	
ail	ank	eet	im	ite	oon	ump	
ain	ap	eg	in	oar	ore	un	
ait	at	elf	ind	oat	ort	ung	
ake	ate	en	ine	on	oss	unk	
all	ead	end	ing	ond	ote	unt	
am	eal	ent	ink	one	ound	up	

Go for It!

1. Make a center, word wall, or bulletin board for rhyming words using these phonograms.

2. Challenge the student to list as many rhyming words as possible.

3. Provide the materials for the student to create games and activities with rhyming words.

Recognize Vowel Digraphs

Digraphs are two-vowel letters that make one sound. Here are some examples:

short *oo*	foot	shook
long *oo*	shoot	tooth
au	haul	caught
aw	squawk	crawl
ew	few	nephew

Skill 10: Recognize Vowel Diphthongs

Rule: Two or more vowels blending their sounds together form a diphthong. Each letter sound is heard when the diphthong is pronounced. The most common diphthongs are *oy, oi, ow,* and *ou.*

Sentence Challenge

Challenge students to make up sentences using words with the diphthongs. For example, "Roy spoiled the proud cow."

Diphthong Glide

Most vowels are short, silent, or long,
But some get together and form a diphthong.

When two vowels join together side by side,
They often make a new sound as they glide.
Oink, towel, grouch, spoil, ouch, and ground,
All are words with a diphthong sound.
W and y become vowels like they're wearing a disguise.
Say growl, toy, wow, and boy to be diphthong wise.

Skill 11: Recognize the Controlling *R*

Rule: The letter *r* "controls" vowels; that is, when the letter *r* follows the vowel, it changes the vowel's sound. The vowel sound before the *r* is neither long nor short. Instead, it has another sound. Here are some examples:

ar	cartoon	partner	yard
er	jersey	mermaid	servant
ir	birth	first	giraffe
or	dorm	normal	score
ur	survive	blur	curtain

The Consonant R *in Command*

The letter r takes complete vowel control.
It makes vowels take a unique sound in their new role.
Watch r command change in vowel sounds everywhere.
Listen to the words star, germ, chirp, work, turn, and there.

Skill 12: Use the Proper Sounds of *Y*

Rule A: When the letter *y* is at the end of a one-syllable word with no other vowel, the *y* usually makes the long *i* sound: *sky, shy, fly.*

Rule B: If the letter *y* is the last letter of a syllable with no other vowels, it usually makes the sound of long *e* or long *i*: *baby, century, satisfy, terrify, terribly.*

STRUCTURAL ANALYSIS

Structural analysis is identifying words by dividing and examining their parts. Word analysis uses root words, word origins, prefixes, suffixes, and syllables. The reader uses these keys to decode, attack, and pronounce an unknown word.

Root Words

Our language includes various forms of words. Root words change their meaning when prefixes and suffixes are added to them. Students need to know how to divide a word into syllables using root words and affixes.

A root word is the origin of a word family (see Figure 6.3). A root word often is referred to as the base or stem. The spelling of a root word often changes when a suffix is added, as in *merry/merrily*.

Figure 6.3   Common Roots

Root	Origin	Meaning	Words
cap	Latin	head	captain, capital
ced	Latin	believe	credit, creditor
cycl	Greek	circle	bicycle, tricycle
deci	Greek	ten	decimeter, decimal
dyna	Greek	power	dynamite, dynamic
geo	Greek	geo	geography, geometry
gon	Greek	angle	polygon, hexagon
ped	Latin	foot	pedal, pediatrician
phon	Greek	sound	phonics, telephone
scribe	Latin	write	describe subscribe
vid	Latin	see	video, evident

Prefixes

A prefix attaches to the beginning of a word and changes its meaning. It is easy to remember the meaning of the word *prefix: pre* means "before," and *fix* means "to place," so a prefix is placed before the root word. Think about *dislike, rework, unpack, precede,* and *preview.*

Content-Related Prefixes

Most subject areas have prefixes that are used with vocabulary words related to the topic (see Figure 6.4). Identify these prefixes and teach them while introducing the topic. Make the list and post it!

Here are some examples from math:

bi	mono	rect
co	multi	semi
contra	octa	tri
equi	peri	
kilo	quad	

Figure 6.4   Common Prefixes

Prefix	Meaning	Words
ad	to	adapt, addict, admit
auto	self	automobile, automatic, autobiography
co	together	coauthor, cooperate, coexistence
dis	opposite	discharge, displeasure, distrustful
extra	outside	extraordinary, extraterrestrial, extrasensory
fore	first part	foresight, forefather, foreclose
il	not	illegal, illiterate, illogical
im	into	immerse, implant, import
im	not	immature, imperfect, imprison
in	not	inability, incomplete, inhumane
inter	across	international, interview, interweave
mis l p	wrong	misfortune, misfit, misspent
non	not	nonsense, nonstop, nonresident
re	again	rebuilt, reforest, reprint
re	back	recall, repay, retract
trans	across	transportation, transoceanic, transatlantic
un	not	unattractive, unclasp, unorganized

Suffixes

A suffix is a syllable with a special meaning that is added to the end of a word (see Figure 6.5). Often the ending completely changes the meaning of the word.

Figure 6.5	Common Suffixes	
Suffix	Meaning	Words
ade	action	blockade, escapade, stockade
ant	one who	assistant, merchant, servant
cle	small	cubicle, particle, article
ic	relating to	comic, historic, mimic
let	small	booklet, leaflet, starlet
ly	similar to	motherly, sickly, worldly
or	one who	actor, doctor, donor

Syllables

Syllables are the parts of a word. Each syllable contains only one vowel sound. The vowel sound and its consonants create the syllable. There are as many syllables in a word as there are vowel sounds. Demonstrate how to pronounce the small parts or syllables and make them flow together to create larger words.

Syllable Rules

Rule 1: When two consonants come between two vowels, the word is usually divided between the consonants: *ex/tend, man/ners, yel/low, fun/gus.*

Rule 2: When one consonant comes between two vowels, divide the word after the first vowel: *re/turn, ro/tate, pre/view, pro/fessional.*

Rule 3: If a word ends in a consonant followed by the letters *le*, the consonant and *le* form the last syllable: *bub/ble, bicy/cle, nib/ble, gam/ble.*

Rule 4: Divide a word after a prefix: *re/construct, sub/marine, bi/cycle, trans/portation.*

Rule 5: Divide a word before the suffix: *teach/er, eleva/tion, tempera/ment, quick/ly.*

Syllable Standoff!

Write the rules for dividing words into syllables on large cards and post them around the room. Assign partners or small groups. Give the following directions to students so they can practice the rules to divide content vocabulary words into syllables:

1. Find high-challenging words in the text with three or more syllables.

2. Apply the syllable rules to divide the words into syllables.

3. Place your words under the rule that divide it into syllables.

NOTE: Keep adding words to form a word wall for reference.

Syllable Sense

Use this poem to teach students how to say words in syllables:

Syllables show you how to say a new word.
Each part is said with sounds you've heard.

In every syllable, in every word,
At least one vowel sound is heard.

Clap each part of a word you know.
Each clap counts a syllable as you go.

You can count syllables with your chin.
Your chin drops to signal a syllable's end.

Count the syllables this new way,
So you'll know little word parts to say.

—Chapman and King

Create a riddle using a word with multiple syllables, as in this example:

Syllable Riddles

I have four feet.
I hang by my tail.
I have two syllables.
What am I? (monkey)

Accent Rules and Clues

Students need to know the rules to decide where the accent or stress is placed. Stressed syllables help the reader pronounce and recognize unknown multisyllable words. Adapt this dialogue to help students understand how accents are used:

If you can pronounce the word, you can figure out which syllable is accented. Say the word in a phrase or in a sentence quickly and listen to which syllable has the most emphasis. That is the accented or stressed syllable.

Rule 1. Prefixes and suffixes usually are not accented: *un COV er, un FRIEND ly.*
Rule 2. First syllables are usually accented in base or root words with no prefixes or suffixes: *A pril, PEN cil.*
Rule 3. The meaning changes in some words when there is a shift in accent: *CON tent, con TENT; OB ject, ob JECT.*

Adapt the checklist in Figure 6.6 to assess the weaknesses and strengths of a reader's phonics use. Periodically monitor the student's progress with decoding skills.

Figure 6.6	The Phonics Dozen Checklist

Student's Name_____ Class/Subject_____

The student is able to

	A	B	C	
1	☐	☐	☐	Understand letters are symbols for sounds that form words.
2	☐	☐	☐	Identify the consonants.
3	☐	☐	☐	Understand that hard and soft consonants make different sounds.
4	☐	☐	☐	Recognize and pronounce consonant blends.
5	☐	☐	☐	Use the sounds of the consonant digraphs.
6	☐	☐	☐	Use the long and short vowel sounds.
7	☐	☐	☐	Apply the rules for final e.
8	☐	☐	☐	Understand that short vowels make their own sounds.
9	☐	☐	☐	Know and pronounce the common phonograms.
10	☐	☐	☐	Recognize and pronounce the vowel diphthongs.
11	☐	☐	☐	Make the sounds of the vowels with the controlling r.
12	☐	☐	☐	Make the various sounds of y.

A. Date:	B. Date:	C. Date:
Observer:	Observer::	Observer::
Comments:	Comments:	Comments:

Summary

Teachers need to assess and adjust their strategies for infusing phonics into everyday planning to meet the needs of the diverse learners in their classrooms.

Introduce the word *phonics* and emphasize the value of knowing how to sound out words phonetically. Phonics skills and rules work most effectively when the students need the strategies to learn new or unknown vocabulary words in their assignments and activities. This content context embeds phonics instruction in the act of reading and writing. Remember to identify words and letters in the text and in the print-rich environment to demonstrate how to apply phonics as a valuable learning tool.

Observe, assess, and evaluate students closely while they are reading and writing to identify individual needs. Remove the fear of sounding out words! Present structural analysis with meaningful and useful strategies, not dreaded events. Use this approach so difficult words become inviting challenges readers can meet by applying the art of decoding.

COMPREHENSION AND FLEXIBLE GROUPING 7

Keep in mind that the simple goal of all reading instruction—including instruction in phonemics, phonics, fluency, and vocabulary—is to improve reading comprehension and to make learning to read enjoyable.

—Marie Carbo

READING COMPREHENSION SKILLS ARE CRITICAL TO THE student's success with texts and related materials in all subject areas. Each student has the right to become a comprehending reader. Differentiated instructional strategies for comprehension can be customized to meet the unique needs of readers.

When I understand what a word means,

I can use it to understand scenes.

When I do not know what the words say,

I unlock the meaning in my own way.

When I do not understand,

I search for clues close at hand.

—Chapman and King

WHY DIFFERENTIATE COMPREHENSION STRATEGIES?

The Reader's Background Knowledge Varies on Each Topic

Each reader possesses different amounts of information about the topic. This knowledge base is a result of past experiences. Learning builds from one experience to the next. In the introduction of a lesson, the individual makes links with prior knowledge. The student may think, "Oh, I remember that!" or, "We learned something about this last year." During the learning, the student applies these memory links. Readers need to learn how to connect consciously to their background knowledge.

During and after the reading, learners create links to their worlds, develop emotional ties, identify interests for further exploration, and conclude how they are going to use the new information.

Interest Levels Vary With Each Learner

Challenge and motivate the reader using the individual's personal interests and strengths to provide successful, pleasant learning experiences. Develop assignments that lead the student to explore and discover more about an area related to the current topic. Students' interest levels affects their attitudes toward reading a selection. For instance, one reader may feel successful with an assignment. Another student may exhibit a negative attitude, a result of feelings of failure before turning to the first page to begin reading. Provide a hook or purpose before reading a passage or assignment so the student is anxious to delve into the text.

Each Student's Ability to Read the Materials Differs

Each learner varies in ability to read the material. The student may be able to read the materials but not be able to comprehend the information. Another student may not be able to read the words because of an inability to decode words or a limited sight word vocabulary in this topic. A reader may be aware of a rule but lack the ability to apply it. Another learner may be able to use context clues to understand the meaning of the passage without knowing all of the words. Yet another student may understand a rule and be able to use it automatically as needed to comprehend information. Each reader's mastery level of comprehension skills and strategies is unique.

Students Use Different Approaches to Understand Information

A reader usually has a preferred way to comprehend passages. For example, a reader may comprehend best while reading the information aloud. Another student may understand the information while reading silently. Yet another may need to hear someone else read the information aloud.

Many times, the reader goes through the motions of learning with the teacher. The information is taught, but the student does not remember it. Effective learning occurs when the student sees a need for the information, retains it, and can apply it in other situations. The power of teaching is in creating this buy-in for the reader.

BARRIERS TO COMPREHENSION

One cause of poor comprehension is inadequate background knowledge or experience with the topic information. A student who has little exposure to the topic may have less ability to adapt the new information and skills than a student who is more experienced in the topic.

The reader may be seated in a place or position that hinders comprehension. This student needs to be in a comfortable place, without distractions or interruptions, to concentrate.

Inadequate sight word recognition, word attack skills, and vocabulary knowledge are barriers to understanding. Often a student learns a skill or strategy temporarily but is unable to remember or recall comprehension skills later. The skills are applied in an immediate situation, but the same skills cannot be applied to a subsequent task. If a learner does not recall facts and details in a selection, perhaps the student has no interest in the assigned topic. This unmotivated, turned-off reader is bored with the information.

Emotional barriers also influence comprehension ability. For example, when students do not believe in their ability to read, negative feelings interfere with the ability to comprehend. A reader's "I can't" attitude is a barrier to comprehension. Students need to believe that they can read the material and understand it using the mastered comprehension tools. The "I can't" attitude must be changed to the "I can," because readers' attitudes affect their altitude, or level of success, with comprehension skills. In the words of Robert Sylwester, "Emotion drives attention, which drives learning, memory, problem-solving, and everything else" (personal communication, March 2009).

From Isolation to Connection

Many students learn skills for immediate use or for the next test. According to brain research, individuals learn when they feel a need for the information. The need to know the information in a passage generates the reader's desire to read and understand.

Teachers build new learning on prior knowledge. When an effective link exists between prior knowledge and new learning, the new information is easier to learn, remember, and retrieve. Teaching isolated facts is not as effective as newer, evidence-based approaches that teach for understanding and a higher rate of transfer of knowledge to long-term memory (see Figure 7.1).

Figure 7.1   Comparison of Yesterday's and Today's Reading Instruction

Teaching Isolated Facts	*Teaching for Understanding*
• Material or facts covered • Fragmented skills • Few links between subjects • Low-level thinking • Few personal connections • Emphasis on rote memory • Learning for the moment	• Materials or facts processed • Skills linked to prior knowledge • Many links to other subjects • All levels of thinking • Strong relations to the student's life • Emphasis on long-term memory • High transfer of knowledge

LEVELS OF COMPREHENSION

Teachers analyze texts and create lessons based on the type of thinking that students need to comprehend. The terms *online*, *between the lines*, and *beyond the lines* assist students in their understanding of the three levels of comprehension. Use the following levels when selecting reading materials and developing questions.

Online Comprehension: Literal

Literal comprehension means the reader identifies explicitly stated main ideas, details, sequence, cause-and-effect relationships, and patterns. An effective reader recognizes the main ideas presented in the text, as well as the supporting details. Use explicit questions and statements like these to identify the learner's understanding of facts and details in a passage:

- What is the capital of Georgia?
- List the events that occurred.
- What does this word mean in this passage?

Between the Lines Comprehension: Inferential

Inferences are ideas that the author implies without stating them in concrete terms. The reader derives meaning from information the author provides. The student cannot find the answer unless the passage is understood. In other words, the reader cannot physically point to the answer of an inferential question. Main ideas, details, comparisons, and cause-and-effect relationships can be derived from inferences or ideas that are not explicitly stated. Struggling readers have difficulty making inferences (Oczkus, 2004).

Ask the student questions like these to check ability to understand inferences:

- How did this person or writer feel?
- What do you think the next step will be?
- What was the author's purpose?

Beyond the Lines Comprehension: Evaluative

Using evaluative comprehension, students are able to identify bias, make judgments, and use critical thinking skills. This includes the ability to draw conclusions, critique, summarize, and predict outcomes.

Use questions and directions similar to the following to analyze a student's ability to use evaluative comprehension:

- Why do you think this information is important?
- How does this major event affect you today?
- State your opinion on the topic.

STEPS TO READING A PASSAGE

Readers in every grade need a repertoire of comprehension strategies to use as they read subject materials. Comprehension can be improved by teaching specific cognitive strategies (National Reading Panel, 2000). The following strategies and activities teach comprehension skills to use before, during, and after reading experiences. The passage preview, passage view, and passage review take the reader through the comprehension process from the beginning of a reading experience to the end. Use these ideas to plan effective lessons in reading fiction and nonfiction material. Readers can easily adapt these strategies for everyday personal and academic use.

BEFORE READING: THE PASSAGE PREVIEW

Orchestrate the brain! The brain stores new information by connecting it to prior knowledge. The way a teacher prepares a student for reading experiences has an extraordinary impact on comprehension. Make a link to the learner's prior knowledge or previous experiences to enhance memory. Ask the reader to brainstorm the information already known regarding the topic before the unit planning begins. These bridges and avenues from prior knowledge to new information create optimal learning experiences, because the brain uses the links to store information for future use.

The purposes, goals, and standards are set for reading the assignment in prereading activities. The student understands why the selection is being read, the essential questions, and the information expected to be gained from the reading. It is crucial to build up the reader's spirit of inquiry! Ideal experiences during the prereading session create excitement, causing the student to say, "I cannot wait to read this!"

Match the Learner With the Learning

Match lessons with the student's knowledge. Incorporate the reader's interests and ideas in lesson planning. Prior to teaching each topic, ask, "Am I using the very best strategies to teach the reading skill based on the student's prior knowledge, experiences, and needs?" This question is answered by knowing the learner.

Choose the Reading Rate

Teach the student how and when to set a reading rate. The reading purposes and the type of material determine how fast or slow the material is read (see Figure 7.2). An effective reader identifies the different types of materials that require various reading speeds. The reader's personal interest, vocabulary knowledge, and level of comprehension influence the reading rate. Consider the student's reading rate when designating the length of the reading passage and alloted time for the assignment.

Figure 7.2 Reading Rates	
Fast Reading Rate	*Careful Reading Rate*
• Easy materials • Pleasure reading • Skimming for main ideas • Scanning for important details	• Directions and instructions • Technical terms • Difficult material • Fact-filled information
Examples:	*Examples:*
• Novels • Television schedules • Telephone books	• Textbook assignments • Manuals • Directions for games

Preassess Prior Knowledge

The next part of the introduction is assessing students' prior knowledge. Teachers can use this kind of assessment to make instructional planning decisions (Fisher & Frey, 2007). The results are analyzed to identify the reader's need. The information for the new unit is selected according to the data findings.

Planning for Preassessments

Planning for effective preassessment is essential. Remember to preassess one to two weeks prior to teaching the unit so the data collected can be used in planning and collecting materials for an individual or group of students. This saves time. Teachers who do not preassess plan instruction that does not match the readers' needs. Remember design plans and use them strategically to meet the readers' needs.

To find the students' knowledge base related to new information, use a variety of interesting and novel assessment tools. Choose effective formal or informal preassessment tools from the selection in Figure 7.3.

Figure 7.3 Preassessment Tools for Class Reading a Selection	
Formal	*Informal*

Checklists
Journals
Brainstorming sessions
Pretests
Inventories
Rubrics
Conferences
Surveys
	Four Corners (see Figure 7.4)
	Human graphs
	Cards:
	  • Yes Maybe No
	  • Often Sometimes Never
	  • Got it! Know a little Not a clue
	Likert scales
	
	       2 4 6 8
	
	Discussions
	Conversations

The 2, 4, 6, 8 Graph

The following preassessment tool provides quick, easy feedback. Write each number—2, 4, 6, and 8—on large, separate sheets of paper. Tape each sheet of paper on the wall, leaving a large amount of space between the numbers. Place a large sheet of chart paper and a dark mark near each posted number.

Ask students to identify their understanding of the topic or main idea in the upcoming passage by selecting the number that reflects their knowledge base, with the number 2 representing a low level of knowledge and the number 8 a high level of knowledge. Tell students to write why the number was chosen, for example, "I chose the number 4, because I know two words about the topic and their meanings.".

Students move to the matching posted number and share their reasons for selecting the number. The teacher asks each group to respond to the following questions or prompts by recording their responses on a large sheet of chart paper:

1. Write the vocabulary words you know.

2. Write any questions you have about the topic.

3. List the facts you know.

The group reports on their findings and celebrates. The teacher uses this information in planning to meet the identified student needs.

Variation

Have the class use the four corners of the classroom to differentiate their knowledge of the topic.

Figure 7.4 Four Corners	
I do not know much about this topic.	I know a little about this topic.
I know a great deal about this topic.	I am an expert on this topic.

Identify Essential Questions During a Passage Preview

Essential questions are open-ended. They are designed to focus a student's attention on the topic and generate higher-order thinking. They create connections from prior learning to the new topic, generate predictions, and lead the reader through the passage. The questions provide purposes for reading, stimulate curiosity, and lead the reader's mind to search for answers. Teach students to use the following steps before reading an assignment.

Think

Think and write about your knowledge and experiences related to the topic. Here are some questions as examples:

- What do you know about our new topic?
- What have you studied that would compare to this subject?
- Have you read books or articles that relate to this information?

Write

Ask the student to write everything known about the topic. You could use questions like these:

- What experiences have you had with the information?
- What have you heard about this topic at home or school?

Explore

Ask the students to explore the passage as a preview. Use activities similar to these:

- Look at pictures, graphs, and charts.
- Read the bold and italic print, including the headings and subheadings.
- Study the summaries.
- Read questions at the end of the chapter, if they are available. This preview tells the reader the information to look for while reading.
- Explore the text with skimming and scanning.

If the topic involves a tricky vocabulary word, ask the students to scan the text to find the new word and give a signal when they find it. Tell them to read one sentence before the word, the sentence containing the word, and the sentence following the word. This strategy teaches the reader to discover the meaning of the word through context clues. This has to be modeled so the learner understands the "behind the scenes" thinking while using this strategy.

Predict

Challenge students to make learning predictions. Effective readers continually predict what will happen next. The prediction may be related to the next word or to the next event. Readers confirm or revise their predictions as they read the facts (see Figure 7.5).

Figure 7.5 Note Grid	
Brainstorming Notes Before Reading: Predictions and Thoughts	*During and After Reading Notes:* Facts, Thoughts, and Conclusions

Ask prediction questions such as the following:

- What do you think the author is going to share about the topic?
- What do you think are some similarities or differences between this topic and a previous study?

Share

Allow students to share information about the topic by posing questions like these:

- Would you use this information? How?
- What do you hope we will do with this information after reading it?

Relate

Challenge the student to list interests or concerns related to the topic with these questions or similar ones:

- What do you want to learn about this topic?
- Are there passages, terms, or sections that are worrying you about the study of this topic? Why?

Brainstorming

A brainstorming session brings the reader's inside thinking outside. The teacher's role is to create a classroom atmosphere where each participant feels free to join in discussions and share thoughts. Here are some guidelines for brainstorming:

- Collect and accept all ideas.
- Avoid comments that judge, evaluate, or analyze thoughts.
- Encourage individuals to piggyback on the ideas of others.
- Post the thoughts on a chart or board for future reference during the study. Label this "Our Brainstorming."
- Praise and encourage all students to participate.

Brainstorming Activity

Step 1: Individual brainstorming

1. Think about the upcoming passage.
2. Write down your thoughts.

Step 2: Partner or small-group brainstorming

1. Form partners or small groups.
2. Share individual lists from the brainstorming session.
3. Ask teams to discuss their thoughts and compile a list of the ideas.

Step 3: Total-class brainstorming

1. Call on each group to share the compiled list.
2. Post each key point on a chart, board, or overhead to create a class list.

Grab the Reader's Attention

A "hook" is a gimmick or activity that triggers curiosity and motivates and intrigues students to want to experience learning. Use this strategy in the lesson introduction to build anticipation and excitement. A special reading, a prop, a part of a music selection, a challenging puzzle, or an essential question grabs the readers' attention and "hooks" them into wanting to read about the topic. See Figure 7.6 for some exciting hook samples.

Figure 7.6	Intriguing Hooks	
Article Hooks	*Literary Hooks*	*Artistic Hooks*
• Props • Costumes • Magic tricks • Experiments • Puzzles • Mystery boxes • Treasure chests • Letters • Artifacts • Maps • Pictures • Posters • Hats	• Mystery words • Quotes • Newspaper clips • Headlines • Riddles • Poems • Stories • Passages • Biographies • Jokes • Editorials • Comic strips • Writing activities • Charts	• Videos or CDs • PowerPoint presentations • Musical selections • Recordings • Songs or raps • Cheers • Musical instruments • Photographs • Paintings • Statues • Role-playing • Character debuts • Dance and mime

Introduce the Reading Selection

Use the following list of ideas to plan prereading activities:

- Preview the material. See the "Essential Questions" and "Brainstorming" sections earlier in this chapter.
- Develop and strengthen incomplete background information.
  - o Give a lecturette containing the needed new information.
  - o Use charts, graphs, posters, and pictures.
  - o Correct misconceptions or inaccurate facts from the brainstorming session.
  - o Connect new topics or subjects with the readers' prior knowledge.
  - o Make predictions to link the prior knowledge to the reading purpose. For example, you might ask, "What do you think the story is about?" or "What do you think will happen in the story?"
- Explain the purposes for reading the passage.
- List standards, skills, and concepts the lesson is planned to teach.
- Challenge inquiring minds by posting essential questions.
- Connect new information to the reader's world.
- Teach the new vocabulary words.
  - o Demonstrate the pronunciation and meaning of each word.
  - o Vary strategies to teach vocabulary words and their meanings.
  - o Go on a vocabulary hunt to find key words. Identify and explain how each word is used in context.

Set the Purposes for Reading

Establish the purposes for reading assignments in the initial planning. The reader needs to understand the purpose for reading specific information. The purpose sets the reader's focus on relevant information, stimulates background knowledge, and creates meaningful connections to prior learning.

Give the reader clear, concise statements as guides to set the purpose for reading assignments such as these:

To learn about	To apply specific strategies
To connect old and new knowledge	To apply vocabulary terms
To locate main idea, concepts, and details	To learn structure
To use the facts on a diagram	To understand the author's purpose
To understand procedures and directions	To answer essential questions

Activity: Create a Sketch

1. Ask the student to create a sketch or simple drawing to reflect important procedures, main ideas, events, or steps as the information is presented in a passage. The sketch creates a pictorial sequence and enhances comprehension. For example, ask the student to do the following:

   - Draw something you know about the information.
   - Design a journal, portfolio, or notebook cover.
   - Create a graphic organizer, caricature, or editorial cartoon.

2. Have the student share the design or illustration with a small group. The student uses the sketches to teach the information.

   - Display the products on a chart or poster.
   - Write two or three sentences as captions to explain each picture.
   - Share the pictures and captions with the class.
   - Display the pictures in a class gallery.

Establish a Note-Taking Procedure

Note taking is a powerful skill that contributes to academic success (Marzano, Pickering, & Pollack, 2001). Teach students procedures for taking notes of important facts to remember. The Dual Note Organizer (Figure 7.7) and Burrito Note Taking (Figure 7.8) are two examples of ways to take notes.

Dual Note Organizer

The student takes initial notes while reading the selection and adds to those notes later during a note review, discussion, or while rereading the passage.

Figure 7.7 Dual Note Organizer	
Notes During the Reading	*Notes After the Reading*

Burrito Note Taking

Fold a paper in three-column folds like a burrito shell. This form makes an interesting, productive journal for the student. The reader takes notes during (1) independent text reading, (2) class discussion, and (3) independent study.

Figure 7.8 Burrito Note Taking		
Text Reading Notes	Class Discussion Notes	Study Notes

DURING READING: THE PASSAGE VIEW

A teacher guides a student to be successful and effective while reading. The student should know what to do to understand the information while reading independently or with others. The goals are to understand and retain the needed information in memory for later use.

An Eye on Content

Teach students to use the following strategies while reading an assignment. Model the steps to use, and display the steps on a chart as a reference tool.

1. *Focus on the purpose:* Follow the directions and procedures to carry out the assignment goals.

2. *Search for cues:* Use visual and context cues. Read the headings and the subheadings.

3. *Place yourself in the scene or passage:* Imagine yourself as a part of the scenario. For example, if the passage is about an object, pretend to be an observer standing near the object.

4. *Self-correct:* If a word or phrase does not make sense, correct it. Teach yourself to self-correct automatically when you read a word incorrectly.

5. *Question yourself:* Find the key points and supporting details. Use self-questioning or self-talk as a guide while reading the selection. Here are some questions you can ask yourself:
   - What is this paragraph telling me?
   - What information do I need to remember?
   - What is the main idea?
   - What details support the main idea?

- How can I use this information?
- What is the author saying?
- What do I need to write in my notes?
- How am I going to remember this information?
- Do I need to highlight, star, or circle some facts?

Spotlight on Signals (SOS)

The author places key words and phrases as signals in a passage to assist the reader in understanding the information and to interpret meaning. Teach the student to place the signals in a spotlight using sticky notes or highlighters. Here are some examples. Add ideas to each list.

More Is on the Way

also	and	another	first of all	furthermore	in addition
last of all	likewise	next	second	too	

Where, Oh Where Can It Be?

above	across	around	behind	below	beside
east	far	here	inside	next to	right

Important Thoughts Are Coming Up Soon

a key feature	a major event	a primary concern	above all
especially important	most of all	pay attention to	remember

Two Things or Concepts Are Compared or Contrasted

also	and	but	either	like	opposite
or	rather	still	then	while	yet

Order, Order, Order

after	before	during	earlier	first	later
next	now	o'clock	then	until	while

The Author's Examples Are Coming Up

for example	for instance	in the same way as	much like
similar to	such as	to illustrate	the following

Quick Changes for Thoughts

although	but	conversely	despite	different from
on the contrary	rather	the opposite	yet	nevertheless

Designs From the Mind: An Activity

Teach the student to use mental pictures, or schema, after reading. Use the ideas in this section as memory hooks. Model this valuable memory tool so the reader knows how to use it to retain and retrieve text information.

1. Read a short selection.

2. Draw a picture depicting important parts remembered.

3. Add captions with happenings and facts to explain them.

4. Read the next passage and add another picture with captions.

5. Continue reading, creating drawings and adding explanations throughout the selection.

6. Think about the sequential pictures created.

7. Use the illustrations as guides to discuss the information with a partner.

Zooming In on Important Information

Highlighting and Color Coding

Use color coding to categorize and process reading information. The purpose is to identify key words, ideas, and details. Teach selective highlighting and underlining using color coding. If possible, select colors that relate to the content study. Color creates a memory hook. Use the strategy often in lesson units so the student knows how and when to apply it in note taking. Here are some suggestions:

- Highlight all adjectives describing a key word, character, event, or steps in a process or situation.
- Select a different color to identify all verbs in the passage describing actions or movements of people or objects.
- Color code key words. Examples:
  o The cause in one color and the effect in another color
  o Each step in a procedure, sequence, or directions using a different color
  o Categories to sort and classify using a specific color for each group

Sticky Mini Tabbing

A student will enjoy cutting sticky notes into smaller minitabs. While reading, the tabs are placed under or above key words or phrases.

1. Assign a reading passage in the content area or supplementary text.

2. Give the student sticky notes to use as tabs.

3. Design the tabs with symbols to fit tasks from the following examples. When the reader knows how to apply the strategy, encourage the student to create a personal tabbing key.

Example 1: Ask students to find the main idea and mark it with "MI" written on a mini tab. Then have them find each supporting detail and mark each with a minitab labeled with "D."

Example 2: Students read the passage and identify the number of steps in a procedure in a process. They create numbered minitabs and place them on the steps to show the sequence.

Example 3: Students draw symbols on the minitabs to indicate their level of understanding.

I understand.	* [star]
I can explain.	! [exclamation point]
I do not understand.	? [question mark]

Variation 1: Tracking My Comprehension

a. At the end of each line of reading, students rate their comprehension using the following symbols:

< = I do not understand, but I can go back and figure it out in my own way.

? = I need extra help with this information.

> = I understand this information, so I can go to the next passage.

b. Read the selection individually and tab it.

c. Meet with a partner or a small group and discuss it.

d. Compose lists of "What Was Learned" and "What I Want to Know."

e. Ask students to share their findings with a classmate.

Variation 2: Symbols for Self-Monitoring

GVI	Got a Visual Image
RA	Read Again
MBI	Must Be Important
LAP	Look at Picture
?	I Am Confused
!	I Got It!

Shape Up

The Shape Up strategy focuses on main ideas, details, or key words. The reader actively engages in thinking while using this strategy. It is similar to the color-coding technique and can be beneficial in all content area assignments. Apply this strategy with notes daily or periodically. Students use their notes from a current study.

1. Draw a rectangle around each main idea, detail, or key word to remember.

2. Select three Shape Up ideas from the identified facts in the rectangles.

3. Partners share their ideas.

4. Each partner circles facts that are different.

5. Partners compile their Shape Up facts to share with the class.

Variation 1

1. Use exclamation points on the key ideas.

2. Use question marks when you need to know more.

Variation 2

1. Use rectangles on the key ideas.

2. Use circles on the statements or sections you question.

Revisit to Reread

Have the students reread the text or topic information. During subsequent readings, the words become easier, and comprehension improves. Vary the rereading strategies when it is beneficial to read the passages again. When possible, allow students to choose the rereading design. Examples of rereading designs include the following:

- Cloze process: Reread the passage and fill in the blanks with important information. (See the "Cloze Process" section in Chapter 3.)

- Echo: Someone reads a sentence. The student repeats the sentence while following the words.

- Choral: Read the passages orally in unison with an individual student, with small groups, or with the total class.

- Partners: Two-member teams take turns reading assigned passages.

- Independent: Students read passages to themselves.

- Read aloud: The reader listens to the teacher, a classmate, a parent, a tape, a CD, or a computer program to hear the passage while following the words.

FLEXIBLE GROUPING DESIGNS FOR READING TEXTS (TAPS)

Which grouping design works best for reading in a differentiated classroom? Think about the sailing metaphor. On a sailboat, crew members work with different individuals to accomplish various tasks. In a classroom, flexible grouping gives each learner the opportunity to work with others according to interests, ability, and social needs.

Effectively blend the grouping scenarios into lessons. Plan reading sessions and adjust the assignments so individual learners retain the information read. Use flexible grouping designs to give students alternative ways to understand and interpret assigned passages and related sources.

Readers need time to work alone and time to work with others to accomplish assigned reading tasks. Use flexible reading groups to differentiate and meet each learner's needs. The following approach TAPS into each learner's potential, allowing students to work with the **T**otal group (T), **A**lone (A), with a **P**artner (P), or in a **S**mall group (S) (Gregory & Chapman, 2007).

T for Total Group Reading

Class Readings

Use the following guidelines for effective results with class readings of passages or special selections:

- Use short passages.
- Be selective.
- Make statements to establish purposeful listening. Examples:
  o When we finish reading, be ready to share three ways to _____ _____.
  o At the end of the reading, you will join a partner to _____.
- Provide a hook or lead-in for each segment of the text. Examples:
  o Read this to identify three things that happened.
  o Read this paragraph to see how the people felt.
  o As you read this, discover the next step in the procedure.

Volunteer Readings

- The teacher asks for volunteer readers. Choose volunteers who are confident oral readers rather than students who struggle with oral reading.
- The teacher and the volunteers alternate reading passages out loud.
- Pause for discussions, questions, comments, and predictions.
- All students follow the words in the text as they're read aloud.
- The teacher models note-taking strategies so students know how to create notes as they follow the words in the text.

Choral Readings

Use choral reading as a novel activity to read information and engage all students. Practice the strategy with a poem or a passage the class enjoys. If content passages are used for choral reading, select information that students need to remember.

The teacher guides the process so students see oral reading modeled and understand the steps. When a class reads in unison, struggling readers join in with confidence.

Use the following steps for choral reading presentations:

1. Choose the passage.

2. Select and assign parts for individuals, small groups, and the total class.

3. Discuss the use of tones and expressions to show emotions.

4. Rehearse assigned passages.

5. Stop periodically for suggestions and interpretations.

6. Read and celebrate.

Variations

- Call on two students to read a few preassigned lines of the passage as a duet.
- Assign a small group to read a section.
- Ask the total class to read a section of the passage.
- Form small groups by dividing the class into front and back sections or between girls and boys.
- Use multiage groupings so struggling readers build their confidence while reading to younger students.

Stage It!

Often teachers use this activity in language arts classrooms so students can read the characters' statements out loud, but this strategy can be used to emphasize content information as well. Choose students as readers of content passages to "stage it." Assign each student specific content passages so they can take turns reading the information. Position two chairs back to back in front of the room with the sides turned to the class. The readers turn and face the class when reading their assigned parts. When the individuals are not reading, they face forward, away from the audience.

Variation

Assign each student an important noun in a selection. Each time the reading relates to the noun, the student reads those sentences. If the sentence is about more than one noun, the students read in unison.

For example, in a geography passage defining and describing various land formations, such as deserts, prairies, and mountains, each student is responsible for one noun. The student who receives the word *mountain* reads the sentences related to the word.

Teacher Voice: Read Aloud

The teacher may need to read parts of the text aloud. The learners follow along word by word during the reading. At the end of a central idea or thought, the students place a finger, sticky note, bookmark, or strip of paper at the stopping point while it is discussed. This keeps the readers focused on the passage.

Students need to hear the teacher's reading voice often as a model. Brief readings of newspaper clippings or magazine articles and famous quotes take very little time, but an enthusiastic reading voice often inspires a student to read more.

Here are some tips for read-aloud activities:

- Rehearse the reading.
- Choose material that is easy to read and understand.
- Model voice tone, expression, and pauses.
- Stop at carefully chosen points to discuss important ideas or details and to make predictions.
- Use taped versions of the passage.
- Stop occasionally to ask students to make predictions. Include cliffhanger statements to create anticipation. For example, say, "I like your prediction. We will find out tomorrow if you are right."

A for Reading Alone

Independent reading develops researchers, investigators, and comprehending readers. Some learners comprehend best while reading independently. Provide opportunities for students to read alone. Each reader selects a comfortable place and position in which to read. Whenever possible, allow students to choose reading materials on various aspects of the topic.

The benefits of individual reading assignments include these:

Develop interest.	Increase knowledge base.
Work on reading level.	Answer a particular question.
Provide choices.	Provide for specific needs.
Invoke curiosity.	Give reading practice.
Develop self-regulated readers.	Develop pleasure reading.

Independent Reading Time

Provide uninterrupted silent reading time daily, if possible. During this special reading period, encourage students to select their own reading material. If they are not accustomed to this reading activity, begin with five-minute periods and gradually extend the time. Students in the lower grades can usually read for 15 to 20 minutes. Students in the upper grades are usually capable of reading silently for 25 to 30 minutes. Join the class to model silent reading skills. Occasionally share portions of your selection to demonstrate your enjoyment and enthusiasm for reading.

Choose a title for the silent reading time or challenge the class to create a unique name for the activity. Here are some examples:

- SDAR: Sit Down And Read
- DEAR: Drop Everything And Read
- SQR: Sustained Quiet Reading
- SQUIRT: Sustained QUIet = Reader Time
- CAR: Come and Read
- RED: Read Every Day
- Rocking Reading Time—Upbeat background music

P for Partner Reading

Partner reading provides students with opportunities to read the selections, discuss them, and process the information learned. Partner reading is particularly beneficial for English-language learners (Cheung & Slavin, 2005). All students usually enjoy reading experiences when they work together with reading buddies. Use an alternate reader if a student cannot read the text so the learner hears the information. The partners should be socially compatible and have feelings of trust and respect.

Suggested readers include the following:

- the teacher
- the teaching assistant
- a taped version of the text
- a peer
- an older student
- an electronic reader
- a lead reader (see "Follow the Leader" later in this section for the neurological impress method)
- a volunteer

Use these guidelines to facilitate successful partner reading:

1. Each person chooses a partner or is assigned someone with whom he or she feels comfortable.

2. Assign the reading selection.

3. Partners find a comfortable spot that is a suitable for thinking and staying on task.

4. Each partner takes a turn reading the passage orally.

5. Partners decide how they will summarize the read-aloud session.

Dyad Reading

1. Pair a proficient reader with a struggling reader.

2. Assign stopping points for students to
    - discuss what they have read.
    - write information they remember from the reading and share.
    - use sticky notes for questions about the information.

3. Tell partners to plot information learned on a graphic organizer.
    - Share the organizer with another set of partners.
    - Remind partners to keep the organizer until the next reading selection is assigned.
    - Begin the next assignment by reviewing information on the organizer.
    - Read the assigned selection and add new information.

Follow the Leader

This strategy is an adaptation of the neurological impress method originally created by R. G. Heckelman in the 1960s. Follow these guidelines to assist a struggling reader with comprehension of the content materials. Pair a weak reader with a stronger reader.

1. Partners read the information together orally.

2. The strong reader begins reading orally in a normal voice as the other student reads along in a quieter voice.

3. Gradually, the strong reader lowers the reading voice. The weaker reader increases the volume and takes the lead in reading.

4. If the struggling reader stumbles over a word or completely mispronounces it, the stronger reader says the word and becomes the lead reader, completing the phrase without stopping and interrupting the flow of thought. The weaker reader continues to read with the strong reader.

NOTE: The struggling reader continues to read using the stronger volume until encountering an unknown word or phrase. When the struggling reader hesitates, the stronger reader takes over the oral reading, using a higher volume. This procedure needs to be modeled and practiced. It builds confidence, however; because of the support, the student does not experience failure and maintains the flow of thought. There are no interruptions to make corrections. This works. Try it!

S for Small-Group Reading

Think Tank

The different members of the group assume the following roles to complete the assignment:

  a. Discussion leader or captain: Keeps the group on task and oversees the assignment or activity for correct completion.

  b. Recorder: Writes the group responses.

The group appoints one member as the discussion leader of the think tank. The leader gives a signal to stop at predetermined points in the passage to ask discussion questions. The teacher provides the questions if the students do not know how to formulate questions. Anyone in the group begins the follow-up Text Talk discussion.

Text Talk

Use the text talk strategy with small groups to work with oral reading of selected passages. Three or four students create an ideal group. If the group is too large, students tire while waiting for a turn, become distracted and engage in off-task behaviors. The group decides how to read the text orally using one of the following options:

  • Vote

  • Use a spinner

  • Draw names

  • The captain appoints

  • Students volunteer

Variation

  1. The teacher assigns each group a question related to a specific section of the assignment.

  2. The students form small groups, and the teacher gives each group a section.
     • Each group reads its assignment and brainstorms the important facts and details.
     • The group prepares a short presentation to showcase the highlights.

Figure 7.9 shows ways in which students can present their passage to the class. Provide options that make the readers' presentations interesting and memorable experiences.

Figure 7.9	Presentation Choices		
Role-play.	Interview an important person from the passage.	Create a computer simulation.	Create a song, poem, jingle, cheer, or rap.
Debate an issue.	Have a mock television show.	Place information on a graphic organizer.	Conduct a fact panel discussion.
Demonstrate a procedure.	Make a poster.	Outline the information.	Create a fact mobile.

Here are some other options:

- Be a tour guide and walk students on the journey through the passage selection.
- Stage a reenactment.
- Construct a diorama.

As the group presents the reading passage, it may be used as a performance assessment, as the students are showing what they know about the information in the assigned passage.

Differentiated Grouping Designs

After deciding whether the learners will work with a partner or small group, a teacher also has to decide how the partnerships or groups will be formed. This decision is determined by the main objectives of the activity assigned. Figure 7.10 on the next two pages shows differentiated grouping designs for reading.

AFTER READING: THE PASSAGE REVIEW

After reading the content material, provide time for students to process information mentally. Model each strategy to teach students how to use it correctly.

Readers need to know how to apply reflective thinking strategies while reading. Self-questioning is a strategy that has been found to have the greatest effect on reading comprehension (Rosenshine, Meister, & Chapman, 1996).

After learners complete a reading experience, they need various ways to make personal links and connections to the information. Teach readers how to apply comprehension strategies to identify and understand key concepts and main ideas.

After learning how to clarify meaning, compare and contrast details and ideas, summarize, and form opinions, readers can select memory strategies for retaining the information. The After Reading Choice Board (Figure 7.11 on page 150) provides opportunities to practice the comprehension skills and strategies.

Figure 7.10	Differentiated Grouping Designs for Reading	
Type of Grouping Design	Formation of the Group	Description of the Task
Knowledge Base	Preassessment data Survey results Teacher assignment	Members with similar needs learn together in a group. The group has similar backgrounds and experiences with the information. The groups are fluid and flexible.
Ability	Teacher assignment Skill test data	Members with similar needs and skill levels learn together.
Interests	Inventory results Volunteers Sign-up for area	The members work in an area of high interest or choice.
Small-Group Discussion	Teacher assignment Volunteers Sign-up for area Random	A team is formed to talk about or learn about an issue, problem, or standard.
Peer-to-Peer Tutoring	Teacher assignment Preassessment data Approved volunteer	A student teaches another student. The best tutors have just had an "Aha!" moment and share their learning process with enthusiasm.
Random Groups	Luck of the draw Numbering Selecting a color Picking a card	"Unknown" team membership adds anticipation to an activity.
Cooperative	Sign-up Teacher assignment Volunteer Random	Members are given a task by the teacher to complete. Roles are established. The team works together and comes to consensus to share and present.
Jigsaw Group	Number off Teacher assignment Cluster of desks	A small group is assigned a section, a subtopic, or problem to discuss, solve, process, and explain to the rest of the class or to another group.
Station Group	Teacher assignment Volunteer Rotation	A group works at a learning zone, center, or station on a task together or individually.

Type of Grouping Design	Formation of the Group	Description of the Task
Literary Circles	Teacher assignment Sign-up Volunteer	Members read, study, process, research, and discuss a text unit, novel, or article.
Debate Team	Sign-up Survey results Volunteer	The team comes to consensus on an issue based on a similar belief system. Each member commits as the group takes a stand on an issue as a unit. The team presents its side of the issue against the opposite side.
Project Team	Teacher Assignment Random Volunteer Sign-up	The team is given an assignment for an in-depth study that develops over a period of time.
Research Team	Survey results Teacher assignment Random Volunteer Sign-up	The team conducts a search through reference materials and takes notes. They gather and compile data and report their findings in written or oral form.
Reading Partner	Teacher assignment Volunteer Random	Two students read a text assignment together. A follow-up task can include creating a product, note taking, discussions, and feedback.
Learning Community Team	Sign-up Teacher assignment Volunteer Random	A team studies and discusses a text, author, or topic of interest.
Analysis Team	Sign-up Teacher assignment Volunteer Random	A team digs deep into an issue, text, or problem and decides on the facts versus opinions. They present findings as a unit of belief.
Author Study	Sign-up Teacher assignment Volunteer Random	A group studies and discusses an author's life and publications.
Problem-Solving Team	Sign-up Teacher assignment Volunteer Random	Each team receives or selects a problem to solve at the school, community, state, or national level; proposed improvements could be recycling or saving an endangered animal. Task with observable results to inspire learners.

Figure 7.11	After Reading Choice Board	
Summarize the big idea and put it to a beat.	Make written predictions based on the information. Share it with a partner.	Draw the sequence of events on a time line.
Create miniposters to display five facts from the passage.	Reflect on how the information relates to your daily life.	Write the summarized information in a genre of your choice.
Combine, or "chunk," chosen ideas on a chart. Illustrate it.	Plot the information on a graphic organizer.	Select the most important information to create a newsflash.
Organize information learned on a semantic map.	Reflect on the significance of the information in a journal.	Create a way to remember this information.

Formats for Reviewing and Retaining Information

Discussions

Discussions provide effective ways to process information read. They interpret ideas, analyze content, and identify how the information is and can be used.

Searches

Search for information to answer or generate questions. Look for answers to questions similar to the following:

- What did I learn?
- How do I link what I already know with this new knowledge?
- How will I use the information?
- What parts of this passage do I need to remember?
- When or where will I use this information?

Repeating

Write the key facts and details in a unique, personal format. Repeat the information over and over until it can be remembered accurately.

Paraphrasing

Recall the information or fact and give it a personal interpretation by saying the learned information in a memorable way.

Creating Metaphors and Similes

Make links and connections with something familiar. Metaphors illustrate comparisons or contrasts. Similes use the words *like* or *as* to illustrate comparisons or contrasts. Here is an example of each:

- Metaphor: The interstate was a gray ribbon winding through the mountain.
- Simile: The meteorite was like a huge ball of fire.

Rehearsing

Provide readers with opportunities to rehearse and make information meaningful by providing personal choices of modalities. Students select one of their favorite memory techniques to remember the information.

Chunking

Chunking is the act of grouping information together to make one item, such as the causes of World War I or a set of vocabulary words related to plant anatomy. In differentiated instruction that is brain-compatible, educators realize all students cannot process and hold the same number of items in memory. The number of items is carefully selected to accommodate individual differences.

Readers need to know how to chunk information by commonalities, patterns, categories, and attributes. Teach students how to take a long list of items and create smaller chunks to study and remember.

Peer-to-Peer Teaching

In a peer-to-peer activity, the reader teaches relevant, important facts and details found in a passage. The student's knowledge of the information is evident in the presentation, as the reader expresses information in his or her own words. This activity generates deeper thought processing. As a result, more information enters long-term memory.

As the reader prepares for this activity, a deeper understanding develops while analyzing and summarizing the information for the teaching experience. Peer-to-peer teaching may take place among students in the class or with students teaching those at another grade level. A weaker reader participates in peer-to-peer teaching with an older student. A strong reader can be assigned as a tutor for a student in a lower grade.

Forming Opinions

Honor opinions. Students can journal their opinions or write them on graphic organizers. The chart in Figure 7.12 is a grid for recording opinions in the following categories: pluses, minuses, intriguing elements, and suggestions (PMIS). Students can use this chart to fit a learning situation in all content areas.

Figure 7.12 PMIS Chart			
Pluses +	*Minuses −*	*Intriguing*	*Suggestions*
I like _____. I agree that _____. I'll remember ____. I am going to use _____.	I do not like ____. I disagree with___. _____ should be changed.	I am still thinking about _____. I think _____. I am not sure about _____.	Next time we can _____. I wish the author would _____. This would be easier if _____.

Summarizing

Bring all the important facts and thoughts together in a summary as the closure. Use the information to draw a conclusion and respond to the essential question. Use the following follow-up activity for summaries.

1. Ask students to record a summary in their individual journals.

2. Tell them to meet with a partner and share the summaries using their own words.

Fact Sort

1. Students are assigned a selection to read.

2. They write two to four important facts (skipping lines).

3. Form small groups to compile facts. Cut the facts apart.

4. Sort and categorize.

5. Consolidate and rewrite similar facts. Delete repeated facts.

6. Share the facts.

ABC Grid

The ABC Grid (see Figure 7.13) gives the student a strategy or process for organizing and collecting important facts and details from content information. It offers Box A for students to record the main idea of their reading, three boxes for the details to support the main idea in the B section, and six boxes for the facts in the C section. Guidelines for the ABC Grid are as follows:

Step 1: The teacher models it.

1. Select or assign a content passage to read.

2. Give each student a blank ABC Grid to plot the information.

3. Provide color-coding tools, such as pens, markers, highlighters, or tiny stickers.

4. Assign a color to each step: A = red, B = green, C = blue.

5. Model the steps on the overhead projector, a dry erase board, document reader, computer, or a poster so students can observe the teacher filling in the appropriate boxes on the grid with the ideas and details. Students complete their individual grids as the teacher models the activity.

6. Describe each step in your "teacher thinking" process to explain the procedure.

Step 2: Students practice independently.

1. Assign a short selection from the content passage for the students to read individually and fill in the ABC Grid.

2. Provide time for each student to share the results with a partner.

3. Call on volunteers to share their results with the class.

NOTE: Apply this strategy in all subject areas. Model it and apply it to various situations so learners see how it becomes a useful tool. Continue to assign small selections for ABC Notes until the strategy becomes automatic for the learners.

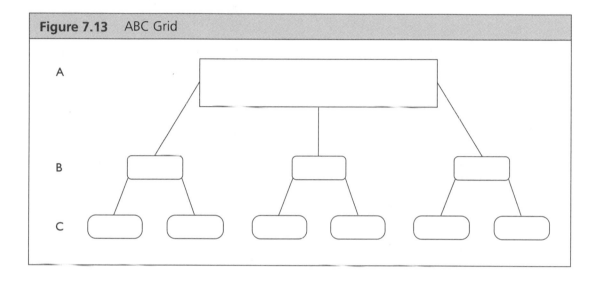

Figure 7.13   ABC Grid

Star Clusters

The purpose of the star cluster activity is for the students to select facts from their reading and organize them on a grid. This strategy teaches readers how to organize main ideas, details, and supporting facts. They use a different strip of paper for each important fact.

1. The teacher chooses a topic from the reading and writes it on a large strip of paper as the topic heading. The teacher keeps this paper throughout the activity to use as a topic organizer.

2. Each reader writes an important, or "star," fact from the topic on a long strip of paper.

3. Ask each student to find one person who has a linking fact.

4. Students with linking facts become partners.

5. Linking partners find another set of partners who have linking facts.

6. Challenge these partner sets to find another linking group to form a "star cluster."

7. The three sets of linking partners stand together.

8. Group develops a heading on a paper strip for the linking facts.

9. Students stand in position with their facts around the heading for a class discussion.

10. Each student tapes his or her fact strip on the topic organizer under the topic heading held by the teacher.

11. While placing the strip of paper on grid, students explain why the facts are in this position.

Music Sets the Scene

In this activity, music is a comprehension hook for memory that stirs emotions and sets the scene.

1. List the major scenes in the selection.

2. Choose appropriate background music for each scene.

3. Make tapes or CDs with short music selections in the order they would play as the background music for a movie.

4. Role-play the main event with the musical background setting the scene.

Information With a Beat

Place important information into memory by using taught facts or skills as the new words for familiar songs, poems, or nursery rhymes, as in this example. (Tune: "Row, Row, Row Your Boat.")

Planet Study

Planets, planets, we will name,
From closest to the sun.
Mercury, Venus, Earth, and Mars,
Now we have begun.

Planets, planets, we will name,
The solar system's for me.
Jupiter, Saturn, and Uranus,
They're the middle three.

Planets, planets, we will name,
Revolve around the sun.
Neptune is the next in line.
Explore the planet fun.

Mercury, Venus, then comes Earth,
With Mars and Jupiter too.
Saturn, Uranus, finally Neptune—
I named the planets. Can you?

—Chapman and King

Misfit Nonsense

A malapropism is a word out of place, misspelled, or similar in meaning to the needed word. The reader uses comprehension skills to find and correct the nonsense error in each sentence. Here are some examples:

- He drank soda pots at the game.
- Many students were absent because of a weasel epidemic.
- She was the couch for the basketball team.
- Jim was the first butter in the game.

Think-Pair-Share-Reflect

This activity provides time for students to process information after reading a passage.

1. *Think about it!* Ask students to think independently about the important parts, situations, procedures, steps, rules, facts, or questions in their reading. Instruct them to jot down their ideas.

2. *Pair it!* Each student reads the ideas and discusses them with a partner. Each individual shares and compares ideas.

3. *Share with a group!* Brainstorm and discuss ideas with the total class or small group. Make a class list, chart, or organizer from the discussion.

4. *Reflect!* Select key points from ideas learned. Jot the ideas on sticky notes. Display the reflections. Teach students to use reflection statements similar to the following after reading a passage:

   - Aha! (The most important thing I learned . . .)
   - I want to learn more about . . .
   - Questions I have about this subject are . . .
   - How does this information relate to my life?
   - What do I like about this topic?
   - What have I read, studied, or experienced that relates to this information? How does it relate?
   - What is the hardest part of the passage to understand?
   - What do I like least about this passage? Why?

Response Journals

Journals are excellent tools to use when processing information after reading. Here are some effective ways to use journaling activities. These ideas and others can be used to create a Journal Choice Board.

- Write a summary, a critique, or a conclusion.
- Draw a symbol or a picture to symbolize the learning. Explain why or how the symbol represents the object or idea in the reading.

- Choose a popular song as a theme. Explain why it matches the topic.
- Write a cheer for a topic or character.
- Design a reward certificate, a medal, or an ad for the group or person studied.
- Pretend you are living in the setting. Write a letter from your viewpoint.
- Write a metaphor or analogy or use other figurative language with the information.
- Compare an individual in the unit of study to an animal: _____is like a _____ because _____.
- Compare a setting to a familiar place: Living in _____would be like being in _____ because_____.
- Compare an event to a happening today: When that happened, it was similar to _____ happening.
- Create a cartoon or caricature.

Boxing Solutions

A Boxing Solutions Grid (see Figure 7.14) allows the student to reflect after reading. Label the boxes to teach the reading standards, which might be like these:

problems	predictions	procedures	facts
identify solutions	summarize	draw conclusions	

1. Fold a piece of paper into four sections.

2. In the A box, state the problem or essential question.

3. In the B box, write your prediction of the outcome or conclusion.

4. In the C box, write the step-by-step procedure or facts.

5. In the D box, write the solution or conclusions drawn by working the problem.

Figure 7.14   Boxing Solutions Grid

A. Problems or Essential Questions	B. Predictions	C. Procedures or Facts	D. Solutions or Conclusions

Act It Out

The readers' unique ways of expressing themselves through creative dramatics enhances memory. Reenact a procedure, story, event, problem, conflict, sequence, or solution by role-playing. Here are some examples:

- Choose a student to be the narrator and assign individual parts to classmates.
- Assign an event to each cooperative group. Have each group act out the happening using the information in the correct order.

Creating a Stage

The following list provides various ways to create a stage for performances. Students show what they know when given an opportunity to be in the spotlight.

- Place a sheet over two braced poles.
- Cut a hole in a refrigerator box to create a performance window.
- Use an old, large-screen television frame.
- Use an old car door and roll the window down.
- Use a picture frame.
- Draw the background setting on a large piece of cardboard or shower curtain.
- Use an overhead projector or document reader that projects onto a large screen. Draw each scene on a separate transparency. Students perform directly in front of the large screen, so the characters' silhouettes project for everyone to see. Students change the scenes as events in the text or story unfold.
- Use four or five refrigerator boxes.
  a. Scene 1: Paint the first scene across the front of the four boxes placed upright and side by side.
  b. Turn all the boxes one-quarter turn clockwise and paint Scene 2 across that side of the boxes.
  c. Continue turning the boxes quarter turns and painting until the last side displays the last scene.
  d. When presenting the play, a student sits behind each box. When the scene changes, each box is turned to complete the scene sequence.

Puppets

Create hand puppets from materials such as socks, bags, or mittens. Use straws, paper rolls, sticks, pencils, rulers, or tongue depressors to form the base for the puppets. Make finger puppets from glove tips or foam balls. Design the puppets to express the look, characteristics, and feelings of text characters, such as historical figures, scientists, or mathematicians.

My Talking Brain

My Talking Brain is an activity designed to demonstrate self-talk for readers. Self-talk guides questioning during the reading process. Teach students the value of using this strategy before, during, and after reading.

1. Select a passage with important facts or concepts.

2. Post a speech bubble containing the words, "My Talking Brain" above the reader's head.

3. The student reads a sentence containing an important fact.

4. The reader looks at the words, "My Talking Brain" and verbalizes his or her inside thinking or understanding related to the sentence.

Teach students to say, "I need to listen to my brain's inside thinking while I am reading." Give readers opportunities to practice this valuable comprehension strategy.

When students know how to apply the strategy to a sentence, encourage them to use it with several sentences or a passage.

Here's an example of this activity in action:

Student: Reads the title for the passage.

Brain: What do I know about this topic? (I am activating my prior knowledge.) What will the author be telling me about the topic? I need to predict what will happen next.

Student: Reads a sentence with an important fact.

Brain: I understand this information. This says . . .

Student: Reads the next sentence and find important facts.

Brain: This is important. I am going to remember . . .

I can remember this fact if a make a quick sketch of it.

I am going to picture this part in my mind.

Student: Reads the next sentence with an important fact.

Brain: I need to find out what this means before I read any more.

Student: Reads the next sentence and interprets its meaning.

Brain: This is easy. It tells me . . .

Student: Creates a memory hook to remember this information.

Brain: These terms are confusing. What kind of notes do I need to take?

I will remember this by . . .

I need to ask _____ for clarification.

Here's another example:

Student: Reads a science assignment about caves.

Brain: How will I remember the difference between a stalactite and a stalagmite?

I will create a memory hook.

Stalac*tites* have to hold on *tight,* because they hang from the roof of a cave. Mighty sta*lag*mites *lag* on the cave floor.

Enjoying Genres and Formats

Use different genres to enhance comprehension and promote further reading on a particular subject in the content area. These sources spark students' interest.

Teach students to use various genres and formats as a part of their reflection exercises by placing the topic information into a selected form. This is a valuable thinking activity because readers use the facts learned and apply it in a new way. Provide students with the following genre and format choice list to demonstrate their comprehension:

Advertisement	Grave marker	Police report
Advertising brochure	Job application	Program guide
Bartlett's quotations	Joke	Pun
Book review	Legend	Rhyme
Catalog	Letter to the editor	Riddle
Certificate	Magazine article	School notice
Comic book	Menu	Science fiction
Diary	Movie review	Short story
Drama	Mystery	Song lyrics
Fairy tale	Newspaper article	Speech
Folk tale	Persuasive essay	Travel brochure
Game rules	Poetry	

Effective Questioning

Use questions as probes to learn what information students know and to identify the information they need to learn. Use the following key words at the levels of thinking identified in Bloom's taxonomy (Bloom, 1956).

Evaluation

select	judge	predict	choose	estimate
value	rate	assess	confirm	evaluate

Synthesis

compose	propose	formulate	assemble	construct	plan
design	arrange	organize	prepare	classify	

Analysis

distinguish	question	differentiate	solve	diagram
compare	investigate	criticize	experiment	contrast

Application

demonstrate	practice	interview	apply	translate
dramatize	operate	schedule	illustrate	interpret

Comprehension

describe	restate	explain	identify	report
discuss	recognize	express	locate	review

Knowledge

define	list	repeat	memorize	name	label
record	recall	relate	tell	report	narrate

ASSESSING COMPREHENSION

Assessment and diagnosis are essential before, during, and after the reading to plan for and meet the strategic needs of the learners. Some methods are formal and others informal. Teachers assess the students' background knowledge related to the standards and use the results to plan differentiated instruction. It is important to know if students comprehend and are able to express their interpretation of the information.

The following ideas are adaptations of commonly used tools to assess comprehension. We have purposefully made these tools quicker and easier to administer than in the first edition of this book. The tools provide instant feedback for use in routine planning to meet individual reader's comprehension needs.

Oral Reading Check

A quick, effective way to check comprehension is to read selected passages to the student. Tell the learner to rephrase or summarize the passages orally using the important ideas. Ask the reader to respond to "who, what, where, why, and how" questions. The learner's responses demonstrate how much the student comprehends while hearing information. Usually, a student who has difficulty comprehending a passage while reading has a higher level of understanding when someone is reading aloud. Use questions similar to the following after someone has read the passage aloud to the student:

1. Who were the people in the passage?
2. What were the important parts you remember?
3. What caused this event to happen?
4. Where did the event take place?
5. Where have you heard or used this information?
6. When did this event occur?
7. Why do you need to know about this topic?
8. How does this information affect you today?
9. How will you use this new information?
10. How would you tell someone this information in your own words?

Comprehension Checklist

Use a checklist similar to Figure 7.15 to assess the reader's comprehension. Use the results to decide if the reader can achieve the learning objectives for the study.

Figure 7.15 Comprehension Checklist			
Skill	Yes	No	Sometimes
Discusses text meaning accurately.			
Analyzes and predicts.			
States author's purpose.			
Identifies the main idea.			
Explains character roles.			
Understands cause and effect.			
Recalls details and important facts.			
Interprets meaning.			
Compares and contrasts.			
Summarizes information.			
Draws inferences.			
Others_____			

Comprehension Reflection Self-Check

The self-check in Figure 7.16 is designed to be completed by the student as a self-assessment of comprehension after reading.

Figure 7.16   Comprehension Self-Check

- Was I comfortable? ___ Yes ___ No   Why? _____
- What can I do if I don't understand the passage I read?
- I need to focus on the passage about _____.
- What do I know about this topic?
- What did I learn while reading?
- How will I review the passage?
- Can I discuss this passage with someone? What would I say?
- How will I use the information?
- Which ideas or details do I need to remember?
- What kind of organizer can I use to remember the facts and ideas?

My Comprehending Way: "How Do I Comprehend Best?"

Discover how an individual reader comprehends best. Conduct this assessment with one student to identify his or her most successful comprehension method. The student may be able to comprehend using each reading method, but a reader usually has one favorite way to learn the material. Use the Comprehension Assessment Checklist to write the results on the Recording Grid (Figure 7.17). As the student orally reads each selection, ask questions, listen to the reader's answer, and record the results in the appropriate box.

Comprehension Assessment Checklist

1. Select four or five passages at the student's reading level or one level lower. After the level is determined, choose passages at the same level.

2. Tell the student the two of you are discovering how he or she comprehends best.

3. Explain that the goal is to understand the information in each passage.

4. The student reads each selection using a different method.

     a. First selection: The student reads orally.
     b. Second selection: The student reads silently.
     c. Third selection: An adult reads to the student.
     d. Fourth selection: The student chooses a favorite way to read the selection from the three methods listed above (a, b, or c).

Figure 7.17	My Comprehending Way: A Recording Grid

Student's Name _____   Date _____

Key

✓	Correct answer expanded
•	Correct answer
?	Partial correct answer
×	Incorrect answer

Forms of Reading	Explicit Question #1	Explicit Question #2	Open-Ended Question #3	Inference Question #4
a. Oral				
b. Silent				
c. Read to				
d. _____				

Student Comments:

Teacher Comments:

5. After each reading, ask two explicit questions based on the selection. For instance, if a paragraph says, "Mary has a red dress," ask, "What color is Mary's dress?" Record the results.

6. Ask an open-ended question like one in the list below to find out what the reader retained. Record the results.

   • What do you know after reading this passage?
   • What do you remember from that paragraph?
   • Tell me what you read.
   • What did this passage tell you?

7. Ask an inference question like one below and record the results.

   • How did the character feel?
   • What do you think will happen next? Why?
   • What was _____ thinking?
   • Describe the scene.

Using the Assessment Information

This assessment shows the learner the best way to read to understand information. For example, if the student comprehends best while reading orally, the information is read aloud. The results assist everyone who works with the reader, as well as the student. The teacher uses the information to plan instruction strategically so the student has opportunities to read orally and reading time is used effectively for comprehension.

The checklist is a record of the student's ability to answer explicit and implicit questions. The teacher uses the information to plan specific comprehension strategies and activities. By using this assessment tool periodically, the teacher is able to monitor and adjust instruction to meet the reader's changing needs during the year.

Running Record

This is an assessment adapted from a reading recovery technique (Clay, 1993).

- Choose a text and a selection of 50 to 100 words.
- Ask the student to read the passage aloud. Take notes as the student reads.
- Place a checkmark by all words read correctly.
- Circle omitted words.
- Add a caret (^) for an extra word the reader inserts. Write and draw a line through a substituted word. Write the word the student substituted above the word in the selection.
- Write "SC" above the word if the student self-corrects.
- Write "TA" above the word if the teacher assists with the word.

Record the results of the Running Record activity using Figure 7.18. The tally reveals the student's oral reading patterns.

Figure 7.18   Running Record Tally Form

Title of Book _____ Author _____ Page Number _____ Paragraph_____

What does the reader do when he or she does not know a word?
Tally each error event beside the observable behavior.

_____ Makes no attempt.   _____ Uses context clues.

_____ Asks for help.   _____ Tries again.

_____ Skips the word and continues to read.   _____ Looks at the pictures or graphics.

_____ Uses letter sounds.

A. number of words _____ number of errors _____
B. words _____ minus errors _____ equals _____ words read correctly ____.
C. words read correctly divided by _____ total words = ___% accurate.

Student Comments:

Teacher Comments:

Student Signature: _____ Teacher Signature: _____

THE TEACHER'S ROLE IN COMPREHENSION INSTRUCTION

Every teacher in every subject area is a reading teacher. The textbook and supplementary materials provide opportunities for students to learn comprehension skills so they can apply them as needed to understand the content information.

1. *Determine how the student comprehends best.* Different readers comprehend differently. Some comprehend more when they read information aloud, others when they read silently, and still others when someone reads the passage to them.

2. *Explore the reader's personal knowledge base* to plan lessons that link prior knowledge to the new information. An effective preassessment is essential. Design questions and statements to activate the student's prior knowledge related to a subject before planning lessons. As a learner relates previously learned knowledge to the new topic, the student makes personal links and connections to the new information. The information gathered varies with each group of students. Use readers' prior knowledge to plan effectively to meet their needs.

3. *Make the content come alive for the student.* Use effective prereading instruction to set the tone for the reader. Provide specific, meaningful purposes for reading and pique the reader's interest using enticing advanced organizers and intriguing hooks.

4. *Provide various materials at individual reading levels and interest areas.* Use a wide variety of resources in different genres at the readers' ability levels that are related to the topic. Encourage students to choose and recommend reading materials.

5. *Provide time for each student to learn, practice, and apply comprehension skills* with a variety of related resources. Use direct instruction for identified comprehension skills.

6. *Use flexible grouping.* Give students opportunities to read the information with the total class, in small groups, with partners, and alone. Plan for discussions of the reading with peers and adults. Group readers in varied ways, using their knowledge bases on the topic, interests, or ability levels. Alternatively, random groupings are effective in most classrooms.

7. *Develop self-directed, fluent, comprehending readers.* All students deserve the right to become comprehending readers.

SUMMARY

In this chapter, effective comprehension strategies tools, activities, and techniques are explored to make a difference in planning for the unique differences of today's learners. Step-by-step guidelines are explained with examples for teachers to adapt to give learners the tools they need to become self-directed readers.

The assessment tools are designed or adapted by the authors for ease in administration, so the results will be available for immediate classroom use to assist the reader. Teachers are encouraged to create assessment tools that meet their own readers' specific needs.

It is up to you to make each comprehension excursion a successful experience for the reader.

PLANNING 8

Learning for understanding requires that curriculum and instruction address three different but interrelated academic goals: helping students (1) acquire important information and skills, (2) make meaning of the content and (3) effectively transfer their learning to new situations both within school and beyond it.

—Grant Wiggins & Jay McTighe

MANY EDUCATORS COMPLAIN, "WE DON'T HAVE ENOUGH time to plan." During planning sessions, be aware of how time is assigned and used. Often the time is used for announcements, individual concerns, and other items, and little time remains for planning.

One remedy is to have all of the teachers report to a central location, such as a media center, commons area, lunchroom, or meeting room, for planning at a specific time. Inform the participants ahead of time so they are prepared to work and stay on task. If possible, arrange for teachers with the same grade level or subject responsibilities to work together so they can share ideas and answer pressing questions.

Administrators need to be present in work sessions. Although they are often overwhelmed with other responsibilities, their physical presence demonstrates support, creates rapport, and motivates the staff. Leaders can circulate, giving pats on the back, providing assistance as needed, and making encouraging remarks. They can assist with distributing materials and keep the teams on-task so the focus stays on planning. It is amazing to see how much is accomplished at the end of the period when everyone stays on-task. Use the following activities or tools to guide planning during team meetings.

A SCHOOLWIDE PLANNING TOOL: THREADING A READING SKILL THROUGH THE CONTENT AREAS

Analyze the reading data, including daily work and test results, and identify an area that needs improvement across content areas or grade levels. Make the selected need a goal. Meet as a group to identify specific ways to teach the identified skills and implement the goal.

Each teacher makes a list of ways to teach the designated skill or strategy to his or her students. Encourage each stakeholder to integrate the needed skill into the subject or grade level over a specific period of time. This team effort provides students a variety of opportunities to apply the skill or strategy in more than one subject.

Reading is a vital component of most lessons in all content areas. When planning each instructional segment, preassess the students to identify their knowledge base in relation to the topic. While targeting the standards in the subject area lesson, identify the reading skills students should have to complete the tasks. Avoid teaching reading skills in isolation. Instead, strategically interweave them into the content lessons using differentiated strategies and activities that meet individual needs.

PLANNING TO USE READING STRATEGIES EFFECTIVELY

Differentiated reading instruction creates opportunities for readers to learn strategies that will become springboards to more advanced experiences. The individual's strengths and interests are key elements to consider when designing customized plans.

The ultimate goal in using differentiated instruction is to teach students how to use their individual strengths to learn tools for studying or reading. A *strategy* is a way to learn a skill (Peterson & VanDerWege, 2002). A reader takes ownership of a strategy when it can be applied automatically as needed in academic and daily activities. For this to occur, teach each reading strategy explicitly. While demonstrating and explaining practical applications of the steps and procedures, verbalize the self-talk, or inside thinking, that accompanies each step. Model the strategy in various situations. Use guided practice sessions until students are able to apply the approach while reading independently.

Planning With a Variety of Strategies

Variety is the spice of learning. Vary instructional strategies so more students retain the information. Identify a key concept and then brainstorm many ways to teach it. Remember every brain is unique, so students learn in different ways. Learners should feel that the content is relevant and have the desire to learn the information. It is easier for students to absorb information when it is linked to their prior personal experiences. When planning, ask yourself questions like these to select the most appropriate strategy:

- Which skill or concept I am going to teach?
- How will I preassess to identify the information the reader needs to know?
- What are the best strategies to use for this individual or group of students?
- What is an effective way to group students to teach this reading strategy?

Remember the TAPS acronym:

T = Total group.

A = Alone.

P = Partner.

S = Small group.

It is essential for the student to become proficient in multiple reading strategies to understand a range of subject material. Use the checklist (Figure 8.1) to identify areas of focus for targeting readers' needs during planning.

Figure 8.1   Personal Tools for the Comprehending, Fluent Reader

- ❐ Use relevant text materials.
- ❐ Use self-assessment tools throughout the reading process.
- ❐ Apply strategies before, during, and after reading.
- ❐ Learn related vocabulary words.
- ❐ Use word attack skills.
- ❐ Apply context clues.
- ❐ Connect prior knowledge and experiences.
- ❐ Adjust to the reading level of the material.
- ❐ Use self-monitoring for understanding.
- ❐ Adjust to personal reading needs.
- ❐ Gather information from the text.
- ❐ Develop related questions.
- ❐ Organize information in a unique way or on a graphic organizer.
- ❐ Create a product using the information.

Design instructional strategies so the student is successful. Involve the learner in planning whenever possible.

Planning to Use Activities Effectively

After standards and strategies are identified, select the best activity or series of activities to develop the most effective reading assignments. There are so many standards to teach and such a wide range of diversity among learners today that selecting the most appropriate reading activities for individuals and small groups can be a challenging task. Use questions like the following to guide your selection of the most effective reading activities for your daily plans.

- What does the activity teach?
- Does it meet the needed goals?
- Where can I infuse the activity into the subject material to teach the learner how to use the strategy while reading the assignment?
- Which students need this activity?
- Do I have the appropriate materials? If not, is it worth my time to gather or purchase them?
- Does this activity use the most effective format for this group of students: center, cooperative learning, manipulatives, folder, computer, worksheet?
- Can the students complete the activity independently after they receive instructions?
- Is this the most effective activity to practice and learn the skill or standard?
- Will students work alone, with partners, or in small groups to complete the assignment?
- Will this activity be part of a class assignment, or completed at home and at school?
- Do I need to include reading choices in the activity?

The Appendix on page 183 outlines each strategy and activity in this resource. Use this tool in planning to analyze and evaluate your implementation of differentiated instructional strategies in your classroom. When a need is indicated, refer to the activity and related page numbers to add to your intervention repertoire.

PLANNING FOR READING OF INFORMATIONAL TEXT

Reading informational text requires more complex thinking processes than reading a story or novel. Readers often think they need to read each word to absorb all the specific information. Students need to learn how to read for the purpose of discovering important bits of information.

Here are examples of informational text students often encounter:

textbook	Web search	dictionary	thesaurus
article	encyclopedia	newspaper	glossary
index	research	manual	technical guide
brochure	directions	recipe	atlas

The following strategies have to be taught, demonstrated, and practiced to become internalized skills for reading informational text:

1. Identify the purpose of the search.
2. Read the introduction or first paragraph of the assignment.
3. Read the questions provided, to identify information needed.
4. Read the headings and subheadings.
5. Read the topic sentence under each subheading.
6. Read the summary or conclusion.
7. Skim the entire selection.
8. Scan for key vocabulary words in the text. If you do not know a word, look for a definition, example, synonym, or antonym in the context that will provide clues to its meaning. The glossary or a dictionary provides definitions for unknown words that cannot be unlocked with the application of context clues.
9. Scan the selection for proper nouns, such as important locations, names of people, and events.
10. Take notes and answer assigned questions while working with the information.
11. Use the index to find the page numbers for key terms.

Teacher's Role

1. Give students permission not to read every word. Emphasize that they are looking for important facts when reading informational text.
2. Teach students to skim the text with guided exercises. Practice this skill often to demonstrate how much information can be gathered with skimming. Adapt this example of a step-by-step procedure to teach students how to skim.

   a. Identify a page for the students to skim.
   b. Assign a brief amount of time to skim. For example, tell students they have five seconds to look at a section or a passage and remember as much as possible.
   c. As soon as the time is up, have the students close the text and look at you.
   d. Tell everyone to jot down everything they remember from skimming the text.
   e. Ask students to share and combine their findings with a partner.
   f. Compile a class list of the responses.
   g. Celebrate the number of items retrieved from the five-second skimming.

3. Show students how to take notes from informational text. Model various ways to paraphrase and record key facts. Demonstrate the importance of writing enough yet not too much information. Note: Tell students to remember that taking notes uses a brief format, but the notes contain the most important information.

4. Demonstrate ways to scan and zero in on a certain word, phrase, or section by giving students specific information to find quickly. Play a game by naming details to locate in the text. Challenge students to see who will be the first to find each piece of information. This is an exciting activity to play with a partner or a team. Here are examples of information to challenge students in a search activity:

date	happening	event	person	place
causes	word	description	fact	main idea
reason	detail	sequence	how to	definition
number	answer	location	picture	chart
key word	graph data	meaning	page number	caption

Student's Role

Students need these skills to be successful readers of informational text:

- Locate information quickly.

- Take useful notes.

- Distinguish between important and unimportant information.

- Identify fiction and nonfiction, opinion, or propaganda.

- Find the most important facts.

- Find key vocabulary words in context.

- Interpret meaning.

- Draw conclusions.

- Find the main idea.

- Identify irrelevant information.

- Make inferences.

To read informational text, the learner exercises purposeful reading. As students advance through the grade levels, they are faced with more complex texts. If students in the early and upper grades use informational text as well as fiction, they are better prepared to attack a variety of reading demands (see Figure 8.2). Today readers of all ages are relying on the Web to locate specific information; skills for reading informational text are as needed in the electronic environment as with printed materials.

Figure 8.2   Reading Across Content Areas

Mathematics	Science	Language Arts
• Solve word problems. • Understand mathematical terms. • Analyze statistical reports. • Follow procedures. • Use step-by-step directions. • Interpret mathematical symbols. • Read math texts and resource materials. • Read charts and graphs.	• Locate and use sources of information. • Understand and use formulas. • Apply data from reading to practical problems. • Follow directions for experiments. • Read directions. • Gain accurate information from visuals such as charts, diagrams, and graphs. • Read for exact meaning. • Organize data. • Research topics.	• Read fiction and nonfiction. • Read information in various genres. • Reflect on learning. • Plot information on a graphic organizer. • Read and follow directions. • Conduct research projects. • Locate and use information. • Apply information to personal life situations. • Learn vocabulary. • Take notes.

Social Studies	Music	Vocational Studies	Health and Physical Education
• Read maps, geographical keys, and data. • Interpret graphics, such as charts. • Understand time lines. • Read periodicals. • Read main idea and supporting details for factual information. • Perform Web and resource searches for investigations and reporting. • Understand vocabulary terms regarding cultures and geographic information. • Compare and contrast.	• Read music notations and interpret music symbols for instruments and vocal music. • Read and comprehend musical theory. • Read music history and biographies of composers. • Evaluate music and critiques. • Learn technical vocabulary. • Read and memorize song lyrics. • Create musical compositions.	• Master technical terms, symbols, and meanings. • Interpret recipes and training and assembly manuals. • Read charts, plans, diagrams, and pictures. • Gain information from main ideas and specific details to make applications. • Learn about careers. • Use safety rules and follow written directions. • Apply directions for projects from journals, catalogs, and magazines.	• Read biographies of sports figures. • Read journal articles and medical Web sites. • Research data. • Understand advertising, media, and propaganda techniques. • Follow directions. • Learn procedures and apply them. • Read training manuals. • Follow play guides.

TEXT CHECK

As our students strive to become successful readers, they need to be familiar with how books are organized.

Present the Big Picture

Introduce major parts of the text so students know the location and purpose of each one. Explore and explain how to use the following tools to comprehend the text. Here are some common components of a textbook and a typical chapter. Adapt this list to teach your students text format.

Textbook Parts	Chapter Parts
☐ Cover format	☐ Introductions
☐ Cover illustrations	☐ Advanced organizers
☐ Spine	☐ Headings
☐ Copyright page	☐ Subheadings
☐ Dedication	☐ Bold, italicized, or highlighted terms
☐ Table of contents	☐ Key vocabulary
☐ Anticipation guide	☐ Lists
☐ Preface	☐ Graphics
☐ Chapters	☐ Captions
☐ Study guide	☐ Labels
☐ Bibliography	☐ Summaries
☐ Glossary	☐ Study questions
☐ Appendix	☐ Review activities
☐ Index	

Analyze the Value of Reading Assignments: Keep the Text or Discard It?

Class time is limited. Productive teachers do not waste it. Examine every aspect of a lesson to determine the best use of the student's time.

Analyze the value of the information by responding to the following questions:

Is the information . . .

- valuable in the student's academic work as a standard, skill, concept, or strategy?
- part of an assessed standard?
- valuable in the student's personal life?

If the answer is no to all questions, consider abandoning the information. Find an effective replacement in supplementary materials.

Identify Deficient Standards

The quality of a school as a learning community can be measured by how effectively it addresses the needs of struggling students.

—Wright (2005, pp. 1, 6)

Identifying Standards to Address With Multiple Students

Analyze the test data and select one to four standards that appear as areas of need or weakness. Write the name of each identified standard on the form (Figure 8.3).

Write the names of students who are having difficulty with that particular area. Arrange students by periods if you teach more than one class. Plan instructional time to meet with the small groups to fill in the missing background knowledge related to the standard. If most of the students did not score well on a standard, it is not necessary to place those results on a chart; teach the standard to the class. If a few students demonstrated mastery of the standard, plan an activity for the group to extend and enrich their knowledge of the topic.

Figure 8.3 Standard Areas of Need	
1. Standard: _____ Students in need of assistance:	2. Standard: _____ Students in need of assistance:
3. Standard: _____ Students in need of assistance:	4. Standard: _____ Students in need of assistance:

Identifying Standards to Address With Individual Students

Figure 8.4 shows a matrix that is a handy planning tool with which to target a student's deficient standards. Identify students who lack mastery in each area to create an instant referral list. In the space provided write anecdotal notes with specific observable comments.

Figure 8.4   Targeting Deficient Standards

Students' Standard	Standard	Standard	Standard	Standard
1.				
2.				
3.				
4.				
5.				

Figure 8.5 can be used by teachers with multiple classes to plan interventions for students.

Figure 8.5 Planning for Interventions Chart			
Standard A _____	Standard B _____	Standard C _____	Standard D _____
Names /Class Period: 1. 2. 3. 4.	Names/Class Period: 1. 2. 3. 4.	Names/Class Period: 1. 2. 3. 4.	Names/Class Period: 1. 2. 3. 4.

Interventions
__ Small-Group
    Instruction
__ Learning Station
__ Homework
__ Computer Lab
__ Volunteer Tutor
__ Special Resources
__ Peer Tutor
Other Services
_____
_____
	Interventions
	__ Small-Group
	    Instruction
	__ Learning Station
	__ Homework
	__ Computer Lab
	__ Volunteer Tutor
	__ Special Resources
	__ Peer Tutor
	Other Services
	_____
	_____
		Interventions
		__ Small-Group
		    Instruction
		__ Learning Station
		__ Homework
		__ Computer Lab
		__ Volunteer Tutor
		__ Special Resources
		__ Peer Tutor
		Other Services
		_____
		_____
			Interventions
			__ Small-Group
			    Instruction
			__ Learning Station
			__ Homework
			__ Computer Lab
			__ Volunteer Tutor
			__ Special Resources
			__ Peer Tutor
			Other Services
			_____
			_____

Ways to Teach It	Ways to Teach It	Ways to Teach It	Ways to Teach It
Assessment and Evaluation	Assessment and Evaluation	Assessment and Evaluation	Assessment and Evaluation
Celebrations	Celebrations	Celebrations	Celebrations

Special Services for Students With Diagnosed Reading Problems

Learners need extra services when reading problems cannot be corrected through classroom interventions. Often a specialist or mentor works with the student to reinforce or strengthen the skills. Parents must approve all special services for the reader. Administrators, teachers, or other professionals may recommend programs to benefit the struggling reader. The following services are available in most schools:

Mentors	Psychologists	Speech and language specialists
Counselors	Social workers	Reading specialists
Volunteers	Resource teachers	Physical therapists

DESIGNING READING INSTRUCTION FOR ENGLISH-LANGUAGE LEARNERS

Culturally responsive instruction is characterized by careful attention to the linguistic and experiential backgrounds of students in order to explicitly connect instruction to those backgrounds, with a simultaneous intention to keep the curriculum rigorous and expectations for student achievement high.

—McIntyre, Kyle, Chen,
Kraemer, & Parr (2009, p. 14)

Teachers today are challenged with the complex task of planning instruction for English-language learners. Standards for teaching diverse learners are identified by The Center for Research on Education, Diversity, and Excellence (CREDE). The following checklists of suggested interventions are adaptations of these standards. Use the items to guide instructional planning for the diverse needs of these learners.

Standard 1: Joint Productive Activity

The teacher and/or learners work side by side using these interventions:

____ Identify instructional strategies to create collaborative opportunities.

____ Designate specific areas of the room for one-on-one assistance.

____ Arrange the room for partner and group work.

____ Use flexible grouping strategies. (See TAPS in Chapter 4.)

____ Form project teams with students of mixed abilities, backgrounds, and interests.

Standard 2: Language Learning

All teachers model and guide language acquisition using these interventions:

____ Provide opportunities for students to discuss familiar reading topics.

____ Listen and respond directly to students' conversations and questions.

____ Interact with respect.

____ Connect the students' language with the content area through activities including speaking, listening, reading, and writing.

____ Give students opportunities to learn content vocabulary using interactive activities during instruction.

____ Encourage and support students in using a combination of their first and second languages during reading activities.

Standard 3: Contextualization

Teachers make instructional experiences meaningful using these interventions:

____ Identify the students' prior knowledge on the upcoming topic.

____ Connect the reading assignment or topic to the student's prior knowledge and experiences.

____ Guide students in activities that make connections with their homes and local communities.

____ Involve parents and families in the reading activities and events whenever possible.

____ Vary strategies and activities to engage the students' learning preferences.

____ Provide opportunities for students to use their preferred conversational styles in responses, discussions, oral assessments, and reflections.

Standard 4: Rigorous Curriculum

Teachers use instructional experiences to move the learner to more advanced applications of the learning using these interventions:

____ Present the whole picture or context of the topic or skill.

____ Design challenging, not frustrating, activities to teach each standard.

____ Plan tasks to move the learner from simple to more complex tasks.

____ Build on the learner's prior success.

____Give clear, specific feedback with recommendations for improvement.

Standard 5: Instructional Conversations (IC)

Teachers engage students through dialogue, especially instructional conversations, using these interventions:

____ Encourage conversations by creating inviting areas for interactions during group work and periods of relaxation.

____ Design lessons to provide opportunities for students to talk more than the teacher.

____ Continually monitor and assess understanding.

____ Encourage students to express their opinions, judgments, and views.

____ Identify the students' conversational styles and use the preferences during interactions.

Developing oral language as well as reading and writing requires having content to talk about; thus, the integration of these areas of instruction and learning should be an inherent part of every classroom containing ELL students.

—IRA & NICHHD (2007)

PLANNING PARENT CONFERENCES: LEARNERS LEADING THE WAY

More parents enjoy attending conferences when their child is leading the session. Design parent conferences as exciting occasions where the student takes a major role in sharing information. Students will learn and demonstrate pride while sharing portfolios, writing journals, projects, a special book, or other accomplishments with their parents.

Here are some advantages of student-led conferences:

- Learning is the focus.
- Enlightening conversations take place.
- Students become accountable.
- More in-depth analysis of the content is used.
- Students take responsibility for explaining and sharing their work.
- More parents attend.
- Parents have a designated time to be actively involved and demonstrate interest in their child's work.
- Students are motivated by the individual attention and praise.
- Each student perceives himself or herself as a learner.

Planning Private Conferences

When a private conference is needed, plan activities to engage the student and the siblings. This allows the parents to focus on the important issues related to the student. This may be necessary during the entire conference or during a segment of the session.

Provide quiet, intriguing games and activities for the student and other children, such as listening experiences that require headphones. If several teachers are conducting private conferences during the same period, consider organizing a supervised event for students to attend such as movies, sing-alongs, board games, story times and play times.

PLANNING HOMEWORK ALTERNATIVES

In classrooms today, homework assignments often become daily routines that create nightmares for students and parents. Too much of the work assigned is busywork. Kill-and-drill worksheets are often long and boring. If your readers are able to complete the first five items correctly, they probably do not need to do all of them.

When students are unable to read the directions or understand information, parents try to assist and often do the work. Parents can lend a hand, but we do not want them to do the student's work. Equally troublesome are the large number of students who do not have anyone to assist them at home. When students cannot complete the assignment, they become frustrated and more confused. We need to think of creative ways to confront and overcome these homework obstacles.

Make Homework Relevant

Give homework a new look! Assign evening learning opportunities (ELOs) so the student becomes a scavenger, researcher, investigator, roving reporter, or detective. These assignments link classroom learning with the use of information in life. For example, when teaching how to read directions, have the students read easy-to-follow recipes at home. Design assignments to challenge students' minds with thought-provoking, meaningful problem-solving activities.

Try these suggestions as alternative names for homework assignments:

ELO: Evening Learning Opportunities	Home Play
	Home Hunt
HA!: Home Assignments	Scavenger Hunt
WLE: World Learning Experiences	Hot Links!
HLL: Home Learning Links	Crazy Connections

PLANNING FOR EXCELLENCE WITH THE OTHER THREE R'S

Robert Sternberg (2008), a renowned educator, recommends schools add the three R's, reasoning, resilience and responsibility, to the traditional three R's of reading 'riting and 'rithmetic as a model to achieve excellence for all learners. Emphasize these keys to academic success in activities and experiences. Refer to these skills as pathways to academic success. Whenever possible, incorporate the other three Rs in your content reading plans and expectations.

The Other Three Rs	Explanation	Examples
Reasoning	• Set of thinking skills an individual needs to become "an active, engaged citizen of the world." • Thinking skills include creative, critical, analytical and practical, and wise thinking.	• Justify • Argue • identify causes • Draw inferences • Support ideas • Draw conclusions
Resilience	• Persistence in achieving goals despite the obstacles in life. • Overcoming roadblocks, working toward goals with passion, possessing self-efficacy.	• Seeing errors as gateways to improvement • Learning to keep on keeping on • Rising above failure
Responsibility	• The ethical and moral dimensions of development including ethics, wisdom, care and the right action.	• Knowing right from wrong • Being accountable for one's behavior • Assuming and carrying out duties and obligations

SOURCE: Adapted from Sternberg (2008).

CONCLUSION

Whatever your role, join in the common goal to guide every student to learn and become a productive, self-directed reader. Embark upon this challenging quest by establishing a personalized curriculum using differentiated instruction.

The power of reading lifts an individual above his or her socioeconomic background, leads to a chosen profession, and promotes successful experiences. Empower each student with reading skills and strategies as a gift that endures for a lifetime.

DIFFERENTIATED INSTRUCTION IS LIKE A SAILBOAT RACE

On the day of the important sailboat race, each vessel is equipped with needed gear. It is in tip-top shape. The crew is ready. The goal is set to win the race. All crew members are assigned tasks they do best. Excitement and cheering are heard as the blast sounds for the race to begin.

The sailboats follow a planned course from start to finish. Along the way, the captain and the crew revamp plans as needed. Everyone knows and follows the guidelines to avoid penalties.

The journey for some sailboats is smooth. Others have obstacles standing in the way of victory. Although all vessels do not win the prize, the captain and each crew member learn from the experience so they can prepare for the next race.

Like the captain and the crew of the winning sailboat, differentiated instruction ensures success. Plan reading strategies and activities to develop self-directed, productive problem solvers and thinkers who are in control of their reading journeys.

—Bon Voyage!

APPENDIX

Adapt the following planning tools as needed for school improvement. Use this form as a checklist to identify areas of need, topics of in-depth study, and to select topics of a demonstration or showcase.

Category	Page	Not Yet	Some	Often	Usually
Chapter 1: Introduction	1				
Differentiation	7				
Differentiating the Content	7				
Differentiating With Assessment Tools	8				
Differentiating Instructional Strategies	9				
Chapter 2: Creating a Climate to Motivate Readers	13				
Designing the Physical Environment	14				
Design a Print-Rich Environment	14				
Supply Ready Resources	14				
Create an Ideal Reading Spot	14				
Designing the Affective Environment	16				
Provide a Safe and Accepting Atmosphere	16				
Motivation	18				
Flow	20				
Attention, Challenge, Excitement, and Humor	21				
Respect	22				
Choice	22				
Self-Efficacy	23				
Celebrate Reading Achievements	24				
A Community of Readers	26				

(Continued)

(Continued)

Category	Page	Not Yet	Some	Often	Usually
Chapter 3: Knowing and Assessing the Reader	27				
Developmental Readiness for Reading	28				
Meet Your Reading Characters	29				
Nonreading Nancy	29				
Word-Calling Wayne	31				
Insecure Inez	33				
Turned-Off Tom	35				
Correcting Carl	36				
Read-Aloud Renee	37				
Silent-Reading Sam	38				
Comprehending Carlos	40				
Five Views of the Reader	42				
Learning Preferences	42				
Gardner's Multiple Intelligences	44				
Sternberg's Triarchic Intelligences	47				
Gregorc's Learning Styles and Reading	47				
McCarthy's 4MAT Model and Reading	48				
Assessing and Diagnosing the Reader	49				
Formal and Informal Assessment Tools	49				
Using Assessments Effectively	56				
The Grading Dilemma	58				
Combining Assessments	58				
Chapter 4: Differentiated Models and Strategies of Reading	61				
Adjustable Assignment Model	61				
Curriculum-Compacting Model	62				
Centers and Stations Model	63				
Project-Based Models	63				
Problem-Solving Model	64				
Independent Choice Reading Model	65				
Guided Reading Model	65				
Language Experience Model	67				
Shared Reading Model	70				
Read-Aloud Model	70				

Category	Page	Not Yet	Some	Often	Usually
Four-Block Model	71				
From Models to Implementation	72				
Agendas and Menus	72				
Reading Learning Zones, Centers, and Stations	74				
Cubing	77				
On the Flip Side	79				
Choice	79				
Chapter 5: Vocabulary	81				
Identifying and Selecting Vocabulary Words	81				
Preassessing Vocabulary Words	82				
Color My World	82				
Meet and Greet!	83				
Mystery Word	83				
Learning New Words	84				
Vocabulary as Vocabulary	85				
Word Discovery	85				
Adjustable Assignments	86				
Twenty-five Ways to Teach Vocabulary	86				
1. Senseless Sillies	86				
2. Box It!	87				
3. Words in Motion	88				
4. Vocabulary Beat!	88				
5. Evening Learning Opportunity (ELO)	89				
6. The Same Game	90				
7. The Match Game	90				
8. Artful Antics	91				
9. Compound Word Wizard	91				
10. It Takes Two	92				
11. Analogy Action	92				
12. Share and Compare	92				
13. Trio Masterpiece	93				
14. Crisscross Challenge	93				
15. T-Toon	94				

(Continued)

(Continued)

Category	Page	Not Yet	Some	Often	Usually
16. Cartoon Capers	94				
17. Multiple Madness	94				
18. Words on Word	95				
19. Five Up	95				
20. Stick Picks	96				
21. Know Cans	96				
22. Stomp Romp	96				
23. Word Game Trivia	97				
24. Vocabulary Sketch	97				
25. Curiosity Collection Corner	97				
Vocabulary Visuals	98				
Door Magic	98				
Base Word Wall	98				
Word Substitution Wall	98				
Ribbon Wall	99				
Vocabulary Vine	99				
Borders	99				
Design Signs	99				
Collection Bank	99				
Give Yourself a Hand	99				
Critter Crawl	100				
Cues to Context Clues	100				
Identifying Context Clues	100				
Strategies for Context Clues	101				
Subject Terminology	101				
Overcoming Miscues	102				
Miscue Analysis	102				
What to Do With a Miscue	103				
Master Multiple Meanings	105				
Student Mastery of Vocabulary	106				
Mastered Words: Check it Out!	106				
Teacher-Made Vocabulary Checklists	106				

Category	Page	Not Yet	Some	Often	Usually
Chapter 6: The Art of Decoding	109				
Phonics Instruction	109				
The Phonics Dozen	110				
1. Understand That Letters Are Symbols for Sounds	110				
2. Identify the Consonants	111				
3. Recognize Hard and Soft Consonants	112				
4. Recognize Consonant Blends	113				
5. Use the Sounds of Consonant Digraphs	114				
6. Recognize Long Vowel Sounds	115				
7. Apply the Rules for the Final *E*	115				
8. Recognize Short Vowels	116				
9. Know the Sounds of Phonograms	116				
10. Recognize Vowel Diphthongs	117				
11. Recognize the Controlling *R*	118				
12. Use the Proper Sounds of *Y*	118				
Structural Analysis	118				
Root Words	118				
Prefixes	119				
Suffixes	120				
Syllables	121				
Accent Rules and Clues	122				
Chapter 7: Comprehension and Flexible Grouping	125				
Why Differentiate Comprehension Strategies?	125				
Background Knowledge	125				
Interest Levels	126				
Ability	126				
Approaches	126				
Barriers to Comprehension	126				

(Continued)

(Continued)

Category	Page	Not Yet	Some	Often	Usually
Levels of Comprehension	127				
Literal	128				
Inferential	128				
Evaluative	128				
Steps to Reading a Passage	128				
Before Reading: The Passage Preview	129				
Match the Learner With the Learning	129				
Choose the Reading Rate	129				
Preassess Prior Knowledge	130				
Identify Essential Questions	131				
Brainstorming	133				
Grab the Reader's Attention	133				
Introduce the Reading Selection	134				
Set the Purposes for Reading	135				
Establish a Note-Taking Procedure	135				
During Reading: The Passage View	136				
An Eye on Content	136				
Spotlight on Signals (SOS)	137				
Designs From the Mind	138				
Zooming In on Important Information	138				
Revisit to Reread	140				
Flexible Grouping Designs (TAPS)	141				
T for Total Group Reading	141				
A for Reading Alone	143				
P for Partner Reading	144				
S for Small-Group Reading	146				
Differentiated Grouping Designs	147				
After Reading: The Passage Review	147				
Formats for Reviewing and Retaining Information	150				
Chunking	151				
Peer-to-Peer Teaching	151				
Forming Opinions	151				
Fact Sort	152				

Category	Page	Not Yet	Some	Often	Usually
ABC Grid	152				
Star Clusters	153				
Music Sets the Scene	154				
Misfit Nonsense	155				
Think-Pair-Share-Reflect	155				
Response Journals	155				
Boxing Solutions	156				
Act It Out	157				
My Talking Brain	158				
Enjoying Genres and Formats	159				
Effective Questioning	159				
Assessing Comprehension	160				
Oral Reading Check	160				
Comprehension Checklist	161				
Comprehension Reflection Self-Check	162				
My Comprehending Way	162				
Running Record	164				
Teacher's Role in Comprehension Instruction	165				
Chapter 8: Planning	167				
Schoolwide Planning Tool	167				
Planning to Use Reading Strategies Effectively	168				
Planning for Reading of Informational Text	170				
Text Check	173				
Present the Big Picture	174				
Analyze the Value of Reading Assignments	174				
Identify Deficient Standards	174				
Special Services for Students With Diagnosed Reading Problems	176				
Designing Reading Instruction for English-Language Learners	177				
Planning Parent Conferences	179				
Planning Homework Alternatives	179				
Planning for Excellence	180				

RECOMMENDED READING

Allen, J. (2004). *Tools for teaching content literacy.* Portland, ME: Stenhouse.

Beck, I. L., McKeown, M. G., & Kucan, L. (2002). *Bringing words to life: Robust vocabulary instruction.* New York: Guilford.

Biancarosa, G., & Snow, C. E. (2004). *Reading next—A vision for action and research in middle and high school literacy: A report from Carnegie Corporation of New York.* Washington, DC: Alliance for Excellent Education.

Caine, R. N., Caine, G., McClintic, C., & Klimek, K. (2005). *12 brain/mind learning principles in action: The fieldbook for making connections, teaching, and the human brain.* Thousand Oaks, CA: Corwin.

Center for Research on Education, Diversity & Excellence. (2002). *Five standards of effective pedagogy.* Retrieved February 1, 2009, from http://crede.berkeley.edu/Standards/standards.html

Chapman, C. (1993). *If the shoe fits . . . : How to develop multiple intelligences in the classroom.* Thousand Oaks: Corwin.

Chapman, C. (2000). *Sail into differentiated instruction.* Thomson, GA: Creative Learning Connection.

Chapman, C., & King, R. (2009). *Differentiated instructional strategies for writing in the content areas* (2nd. ed). Thousand Oaks, CA: Corwin.

Chen, C., Kyle, D. W., & McIntyre, E. (2008). Helping teachers work effectively with English learners and other families. *School Community Journal, 18*(1), 7–20.

Csikszentmihalyi, M. (1997). *Creativity: Flow and the psychology of discovery and invention.* New York: Harper Collins.

Dalton, S. S. (2008). *Five standards for effective teaching: How to succeed with all learners.* San Franscisco: Jossey-Bass.

Fink, E., & Samuels, S. J. (Eds.). (2007). *Inspiring reading success: Interest and motivation in an age of high-stakes testing.* Newark, DE: International Reading Association.

Gallagher, K. (2003). *Reading reasons: Motivational mini-lessons for middle and high school.* Portland, ME: Stenhouse.

Gay, G. (2002). Preparing for culturally responsible teaching. *Journal of Teacher Education, 53,* 106–116.

Gregory, G. H., & Chapman, C. (2002a). *Differentiating instruction to meet the needs of all learners: Elementary edition.* Sandy, UT: Teach Stream/Video Journal of Education.

Gregory, G. H., & Chapman, C. (2002b). *Differentiating instruction to meet the needs of all learners: Secondary edition.* Sandy, UT: Teach Stream/Video Journal of Education.

Kellaher, K. (2006). *Building comprehension: Reading passages with high-interest practice activities.* New York: Scholastic.

McEwan, E. K. (2007). *40 ways to support struggling readers in content classroooms, grades 6–12.* Thousand Oaks, CA: Corwin.

Siegler, R. S. (2004). *Children's thinking* (4th ed.). Upper Saddle River, NJ: Prentice Hall.

REFERENCES

Assor, A., Kaplan, H., & Roth, G. (2002). Choice is good, but relevance is excellent: Autonomy-enhancing and suppressing teacher behaviors predicting students' engagement in schoolwork. *British Journal of Educational Psychology, 72,* 261–278.

Bandura, A. (1997). *Self-efficacy: The exercise of control.* New York: W. H. Freeman.

Baumann, J. F., Hoffman, J. V., Moon, J., & Duffy-Hester, A. M. (1998). Where are teachers' voices in the phonics/whole language debate? Results from a survey of U.S. elementary classroom teachers. *Reading Teacher, 51*(8), 636–650.

Bloom, B. S. (Ed.). (1956). *Taxonomy of educational objectives: Book 1. Cognitive domain.* New York: David McKay.

Burchers, S., Burchers, M., & Burchers, B. (1996). *Vocabulary cartoons: Building an educated vocabulary with visual mnemonics* (3rd ed.). Punta Gorda, FL: New Monic Books.

Carbo, M. (2007). *Becoming a great teacher of reading: Achieving high rapid reading gain with powerful, differentiated strategies.* Thousand Oaks, CA: Corwin.

Chapman, C., & King, R. (2008). *Differentiated instructional management: Work smarter, not harder.* Thousand Oaks, CA: Corwin.

Chapman, C., & King, R. (2009). *Test success in the brain-compatible classroom.* Thousand Oaks, CA: Corwin.

Cheung, A., & Slavin, R. E. (2005). *Effective reading programs for English language learners and other language-minority students.* Baltimore, MD: Success for All Foundation.

Clay, M. (1993). *Reading recovery: A guidebook for teachers in training.* Portsmouth, NH: Heinemann.

Csikszentmihalyi, M. (1990). *Flow.* New York: Harper and Row.

Fisher, D., & Frey, N. (2007). *Checking for understanding: Formative assessment techniques for your classroom.* Alexandria, VA: Association for Supervision and Curriculum Development.

Flippo, R. F. (2001). *Reading researchers in search of common ground.* Newark, DE: International Reading Association.

Fogarty, R. (2007). *Literacy matters: Strategies every teacher can use* (2nd ed.). Thousand Oaks, CA: Corwin.

Freeman, W., & Scheidecker, D. (2009). *Becoming a legendary teacher: To instruct and inspire.* Thousand Oaks, CA: Corwin.

Gardner, H. (1983). *Frames of mind: The theory of multiple intelligences.* New York: Basic Books.

Gipe, J. P. (2002). *Multiple paths to literacy: Classroom techniques for struggling readers* (5th ed.). Upper Saddle River, NJ: Merrill Prentice Hall.

Glasser, W. (1990). *The quality school: Managing students without coercion.* New York: Perennial Library.

Glasser, W. (1998). *Choice theory in the classroom.* New York: HarperPerennial.

Goodman, Y. M. (1998). Miscue analysis for classroom teachers: Some history and some procedures. In C. Weaver (Ed.), *Practicing what we know: Informed reading instruction* (pp. 226–236). Urbana, IL: National Council of Teachers of English. (ERIC Document Reproduction Service No. ED461098)

Gray, W. S. (1937). The nature and organization of basic instruction in reading. In G. M. Whipple (Ed.), *The thirty-sixth year book of the National Society for the Study of Education: Part I. The teaching of reading: A second report* (pp. 65–131). Bloomington, IN: Public School.

Gregorc, A. F. (1985). *Inside styles: Beyond the basics: Questions and answers on style.* Maynard, MA: Gabriel Systems.

Gregory, G. H., & Chapman, C. (2007). *Differentiated instructional strategies: One size doesn't fit all.* Thousand Oaks, CA: Corwin.

Guthrie, J. T. (Ed.). (2008). *Engaging adolescents in reading.* Thousand Oaks, CA: Corwin.

Guthrie, J. T., Wigfield, A., & Von Secker, C. (2000). Effects of integrated instruction on motivation and strategy use in reading. *Journal of Educational Psychology, 92,* 331–341.

International Reading Association & National Institute of Child Health and Human Development. (2007). *Key issues and questions in English language learners literacy research* (p.4.). Retrieved June 10, 2009, from http://146.145.202.164/downloads/resources/ELL_paper_071022.pdf.

Jensen, E. (2008). *Brain-based learning: The new paradigm of teaching* (2nd ed.). Thousand Oaks, CA: Corwin.

Kauchak, D. P., & Eggen, P. (2007). *Learning and teaching: Research-based methods* (5th ed.). Boston: Allyn & Bacon.

Levine, M. (2002). *A mind at a time.* New York: Simon and Schuster.

Marzano, R. (2004). *Building background knowledge for academic achievement: Research on what works in schools.* Alexandria, VA: Association for Supervision and Curriculum Development.

Marzano, R., Pickering, D., & Pollack, J. (2001). *Classroom instruction that works: Research-based strategies for increasing student achievement.* Alexandria, VA: ASCD.

McCarthy, B., & McCarthy, D. (2006). *Teaching around the 4MAT cycle.* Thousand Oaks, CA: Corwin.

McIntyre, E., Kyle, D. W., Chen, C.-T., Kraemer, J., & Parr, J. (2009). *6 principles for teaching: English language learners in all classrooms.* Thousand Oaks: Corwin.

National Reading Panel. (2000). *Report of the National Reading Panel: Teaching children to read: An evidence-based assessment of the scientific research literature on reading and its implications for reading instruction.* Rockville, MD: National Institute of Child Health and Human Development.

Oczkus, L. (2004). *Super 6 comprehension strategies.* Norwood, MA: Christopher-Gordon.

Peterson, D., & VanDerWege, C. (2002). Guiding children to be strategic readers. *Phi Delta Kappan, 83*(6), 437–439.

Piaget, J. (1952). *The origins of intelligence in children.* New York: International Universities Press.

Renzulli, J. S., Leppien, J. H., & Hayes, T. S. (2000). *The multiple menu model: A practical guide for developing differentiated curriculum.* Mansfield Center, CT: Creative Learning Press.

Rosenshine, B., Meister, C., & Chapman, S. (1996). Teaching students to generate questions: A review of the intervention studies. *Review of Educational Research, 66,* 181–221.

Sheldon, K. M., Elliot, A. J., Kim, Y., & Kasser, T. (2001). What is satisfying about satisfying events? Testing 10 candidate psychological needs. *Journal of Personality and Social Psychology, 80,* 325–339.

Sousa, D. (2005). *How the brain learns* (3rd ed.). Thousand Oaks, CA: Corwin.

Sprenger, M. (1999). *Learning and memory: The brain in action.* Alexandria, VA: Association for Supervision and Curriculum Development.

Sternberg, R. (2008). Excellence for all: There's more to excellence than reading, writing and arithmetic. *Educational Leadership,* 66(2), 14–19.

Sternberg, R. J., & Grigorenko, E. (2007). *Teaching for successful intelligence: To increase student learning and achievement* (2nd ed.). Thousand Oaks, CA: Corwin.

Stipek, D. J. (1996). Motivation and instruction. In D. C. Berliner & R. C. Calfee (Eds.), *Handbook of educational psychology* (pp. 85–113). New York: Macmillan.

Strong, R. W., Silver, H. F., Perini, M. J., & Tuculescu, G. M. (2002). *Reading for academic success: Powerful strategies for struggling, average, and advanced readers, grades 7–12.* Thousand Oaks, CA: Corwin.

Tomlinson, C. A. (1999). *The differentiated classroom: Responding to the needs of all learners.* Alexandria, VA: Association for Supervision and Curriculum Development.

Tomlinson, C. A. (2001). *How to differentiate instruction in mixed-ability classrooms* (2nd ed.). Alexandria, VA: Association for Supervision and Curriculum Development.

Tomlinson, C. A., Kaplan, S. N., Renzulli, J. S., Purcell, J., Leppien, J., & Burns, D. (2002). *The parallel curriculum: A design to develop high potential and challenge high-ability learners.* Thousand Oaks, CA: Corwin.

Trelease, J. (2001). *The read-aloud handbook* (5th ed.). New York: Penguin.

Wiggins, G., & McTighe, J. (2008). Put understanding first. *Educational Leadership,* 65(8), 36–41.

Wolk, Steven. (2008). Joy in school: Joyful learning can flourish in school if you give joy a chance. *Educational Leadership,* 66(1), 8–14.

Wright, J. (2005). Five interventions that work. *NAESP Leadership Compass,* 2(4), 1, 6.

INDEX

ABC Grid, 152–153
Ability group design, 148 (figure)
Abstract/random learning style, 48 (figure)
Abstract/sequential learning style, 48 (figure)
Accent rules and clues, 122
Act It Out activity, 157
Adjustable assignment model, 61–62
    for language experience, 69
    vocabulary, 86
Affective environment, 16–25
Agendas and menus, 72–74, 75 (figure)
Alphabet Animals, 110–111
Analogy Action activity, 92
Analysis
    miscue, 102, 103 (figure)
    teams, 149 (figure)
Analytical readers, 48–49 (figure)
Artful Antics activity, 91
Assessment tools, 8–9
    Cloze process, 52
    Color My World, 82
    combining, 58–59
    comprehension, 52, 160–164
    for developing eager, fluent readers, 41
    effective use of, 55–56
    formal and informal, 49–54, 55 (figure), 59
    grading and, 58–59
    guided reading, 67
    informal reading inventories (IRIs), 51–52
    mastered vocabulary, 106
    Meet and Greet!, 83
    Mystery Word, 83–84
    oral reading check, 160–161
    surveys and inventories for, 53–54, 55 (figure)
    vocabulary level, 51–52, 82–84
    See also Diagnosis
Assignments, adjustable, 61–62
    for language experience, 69
    vocabulary, 86
Assor, A., 19
Atmosphere, safe and accepting, 16–18
Attention, 21–22, 133–134
Auditory learners, 37–38
Author studies, 149 (figure)

Bandura, A., 23
Base Word Wall, 98
Behaviors, reading
    comprehension and fluent, 40
    correcting, 36

insecure readers, 33
    nonreaders, 29
    read-aloud, 37
    silent, 39
    turned-off readers, 35
    word-calling, 31
Beliefs, student, 54 (figure)
Bibliotherapy, 16
Blends, consonant, 113
Bloom, B., 159
Boards, choice, 22–23, 85, 150 (figure)
Bodily/kinesthetic intelligence, 45–46 (figure)
Borders, 99
Boxing Solutions Grid, 156
Box It! activity, 87, 88 (figure)
Brainstorming, 133
Burrito note taking, 136

Camouflaged Consonants, 112
Carbo, Marie, 27, 125
Cartoon Capers activity, 94
Celebrating reading achievements, 24–25
Center for Research on Education, Diversity, and
    Excellence (CREDE), 177
Centers and stations model, 63, 74–77
Challenge, 21–22
Chapman, C., 7, 8, 9, 61, 74, 154
    on motivation, 13
    on reading comprehension, 125
    on syllables, 122
    on vocabulary, 81, 88, 89
Chapman, S., 147
Chen, C.-T., 177
Cheung, A., 144
Choices in learning activities, 22–23, 35–36, 79, 80
    (figure)
Choral reading, 140, 142
Chunking, 151
Class readings, 141
Classroom environments
    affective environment in, 16–25
    attention, challenge, excitement, and humor in, 21–22
    building self-efficacy in, 23–24
    celebrating reading achievements in, 24–25
    choices in, 22–23
    for developing eager, fluent readers, 42
    empathy in, 17
    errors viewed as learning opportunities in, 16
    ideal reading spots in, 14–16
    inviting, 13

motivation in, 18–19, 20 (figure)
physical environment in, 14–16
print-rich, 14
rapport, 17–18
ready resources supplied in, 14
respect in, 22
safe and accepting atmosphere in, 16–18
team spirit, 16
Clay, M., 102, 164
Cloze process, 52, 140
Clues, context, 100–101
Clusters, star, 153–154
Coding, color, 138
Coin study, 89
Collection Bank, 99
Color-coded folders/activities, 76 (figure)
Color coding, 138
Color My World assessment tool, 82
Comfort level, student, 54 (figure)
Commonsense readers, 49 (figure)
Compound Word Wizard activity, 91
Comprehension
    ABC Grid and, 152–153
    Act It Out activity, 157
    assessing, 52, 160–164
    assessment checklist, 162–164
    barriers to, 126–127
    Boxing Solutions Grid, 156
    brainstorming and, 133
    checklist, 161
    chunking and, 151
    effective questioning and, 159–160
    essential questions and, 131–133
    evaluative, 128
    eye on content and, 136–137
    fact sort and, 152
    flexible grouping designs for, 5, 141–147
    fluency and, 40, 50 (figure), 169 (figure)
    and formats for reviewing and retaining information,
        150–151
    forming opinions and, 151
    genres and formats and, 159
    grabbing the reader's attention and, 133–134
    independent reading and, 143–144
    inferential, 128
    instruction, teacher's role in, 164–166
    introducing reading selections and, 134
    levels of, 127–128
    literal, 128
    mental pictures and, 138
    misfit nonsense and, 155
    music and, 154
    My Talking Brain activity, 158–159
    note-taking and, 135–136
    peer-to-peer teaching and, 148 (figure), 151
    preassessments, 130
    previewing and, 129–136
    during reading, 136–140
    reflection self-check, 162
    rereading and, 140
    response journals and, 155–156
    setting purposes for reading and, 135

Shape Up strategy for, 139–140
    small-group reading and, 146–147
    Spotlight on Signals (SOS) and, 137
    star clusters and, 153–154
    and steps to reading a passage, 128–129
    strategies differentiation, 125–126
    summarizing and, 152
    tasks and multiple intelligences, 46 (figure)
    Think-Pair-Share-Reflect activity, 155
    total group reading and, 141–143
    zooming in on important information for, 138–140
Concrete/random learning style, 48 (figure)
Concrete/sequential learning style, 48 (figure)
Conferences, parent, 179
Consonants
    blends, 113
    diagraphs, 114–115
    hard and soft, 111–113
    identifying, 111
Constructivist learning, 6–7
Content
    comprehension and focus on, 136–137
    differentiation, 7–8
    reading across areas of, 173 (figure)
    -related prefixes, 119–120
Context clues, cues to, 100–101
Contextualization, 178
Controlling *R,* 118
Cooperative groups, 148 (figure)
Correcting behaviors, 36–37
Crisscross Challenge activity, 93–94
Critter Crawl, 100
Csikszentmihalyi, M., 20
Cubing, 77–78
Cues to context clues, 100–101
Curiosity Collection Corner activity, 97
Curriculum
    assessing/revamping, 11
    -compacting model, 62–63
    English-language learners and, 178
    students and reading, 10
    teachers guiding, 10

Data-driven decisions, 5–6
Debate teams, 149 (figure)
Decoding, 109
    See also Phonics
Deficient standards, identifying, 174–175, 176 (figure)
Design Signs, 99
Developmental readiness for reading, 28
Diagnosis
    comprehension and fluent reading, 40
    correcting behaviors, 36–37
    for developing eager, fluent readers, 41
    insecure students, 34–35
    nonreading students, 30–31
    read-aloud students, 38
    reader, 49–58
    silent reading, 39
    turned-off students, 35–36
    word-calling students, 31–32
    See also Assessment tools

Diagraphs, consonant, 114–115
Differentiated instruction. *See* Instructional strategies
Differentiated Instructional Management, 61
Differentiation
    with assessment tools, 8–9
    comprehension strategies, 125–126
    content, 7–8
    grouping designs, 147, 148–149 (figure)
    instructional strategies, 9–10
    like a sailboat race, 181
Digging Diagraph activity, 114
Diphthong Glide, 117–118
Discovery, word, 85–86
Diversity of students, 27–28
Door Magic, 98
Dual note organizer, 135
Dyad reading, 145
Dynamic readers, 49 (figure)

Echoing, 140
Eggen, P., 6
Elliot, A. J., 18
Emerging readers, 50 (figure)
Emotional barriers to learning, 34–35
Empathy, 17
English-language learners, 177–178
Errors
    letter sound recognition, 103–104
    viewed as learning opportunities, 16
Essential questions, 131–133
Evaluative comprehension, 128
Evening Learning Opportunities (ELOs), 89–90, 180
Excellence, planning for, 180–181
Excitement, 21–22

Fact sort, 152
Feelings, student
    comprehension and fluent, 40
    correcting behaviors and, 36
    insecure, 33
    nonreading, 29–30
    reading aloud and, 37
    silent, 39
    turned-off, 35
    word-calling, 31
Fisher, D., 129
Five Up activity, 95–96
Flexible grouping designs, 5, 141–147, 166
    differentiation, 147, 148–149 (figure)
Flippo, Rona F., 59
Flip side card game, 79
Flow, 20–21
Fluent readers, 40, 50 (figure), 169 (figure)
    developing, 40–42
Fogarty, R., 56
Folders, color-coded, 76 (figure)
Follow the Leader strategy, 145
Formal assessment tools,
    49–54, 55 (figure), 59
Forming opinions, 151
Four-block model, 71, 72 (figure)
4MAT models, 48, 49 (figure)

Freeman, W., 26
Frey, N., 129

Gardner, Howard, 6, 44
Genres and formats, 159
Gipe, J. P., 82
Give Yourself a Hand, 99–100
Glasser, William, 19, 20 (figure)
Goodman, Yetta, 102
Goofy Collage, 111–112
Grading
    dilemma, 58–59
    showcase scoring, 58
Gray, W. S., 181
Gregorc, Anthony, 47, 48 (figure)
Gregory, G. H., 7
Grigerenko, E., 47
Grouping, flexible. *See* Flexible grouping designs
Guided reading model, 65–67
    four-block model and, 72 (figure)
Guthrie, J. T., 18, 42

Hands-on centers, 63
Hayes, T. S., 62
Heckelman, R. G., 145
Higher-order thinking activities, 40
Highlighting, 138
Home environment survey, 55 (figure)
Homework alternatives, 179–180
Hooks, 133–134
Humor, 21–22

Identification and selection of vocabulary words, 81–82
Imaginative readers, 48–49 (figure)
Inclusion, 6
Independent choice reading model, 65
    four-block model and, 72 (figure)
Independent reading assignments, 143–144
Individual Education Programs (IEPs), 5
Individual Learning Plans (ILPs), 5, 57 (figure)
Inferential comprehension, 128
Informal assessment tools, 49–54, 55 (figure)
Informal reading inventories (IRIs), 51–52
Informational text, planning for reading of, 170–172,
    173 (figure)
Insecure students, 33–35
Insertions, letter, 104
Instructional conversations (IC), 178
Instructional strategies
    adjustable assignment model, 61–62
    agendas and menus, 72–74, 75 (figure)
    Analogy Action, 92
    Artful Antics, 91
    Box It!, 87, 88 (figure)
    Cartoon Capers, 94
    centers and stations model, 63, 74–77
    choice boards, 22–23, 85
    choice in, 22–23, 35–36, 79, 80 (figure)
    Compound Word Wizard, 91
    comprehension, 151–160
    consonants, 110–115
    Crisscross Challenge, 93–94

cubing, 77–78
Curiosity Collection Corner, 97
curriculum-compacting model, 62–63
for developing eager, fluent readers, 41
differentiating, 9–10
effective practices and related research on, 5–7
Evening Learning Opportunity (ELO), 89–90, 180
Five Up, 95–96
flexible grouping designs, 5, 141–143, 166
flip side card game, 79
four-block model, 71, 72 (figure)
guided reading model, 65–67
independent choice reading model, 65
independent reading time, 143–144
It Takes Two, 92
Know Cans, 96
language experience model, 67–69
Match Game, 90–91
from models to implementation of,
    72–79, 80 (figure)
Multiple Madness, 94
partner reading, 140, 144–145, 149 (figure)
preparation for, 1–2
problem-based model, 64
project-based models, 63–64
read-aloud model, 70–71
Same Game, 90
scaffolding, 41
Senseless Sillies, 86–87
Share and Compare, 92–93
shared reading model, 70
small-group reading, 146–147, 148 (figure)
Stick Picks, 96
Stomp Romp, 96–97
total group reading, 141–143
Trio Masterpiece, 93
T-Toon, 94
variety, 168–169
vocabulary, 86–97
Vocabulary Beat!, 88–89
Vocabulary Sketch activity, 97
vocabulary visuals, 98–100
vowels, 115–118
word discovery, 85–86
Word Game Trivia, 97
Words in Motion, 88
Words on Word, 95
Intelligences
    multiple, 6, 44, 45–46 (figure)
    triarchic, 47
Interests group design, 148 (figure)
Interest surveys, 53 (figure), 55 (figure)
Internet sources and software, 77
Interpersonal intelligence, 45–46 (figure)
Interventions, 5
    comprehension and fluent readers, 40
    correcting behaviors, 36–37
    insecure students, 34–35
    nonreading students, 30
    planning for, 176 (figure)
    read-aloud students, 38
    silent reading, 39

    turned-off students, 35–36
    word-calling students, 31–32
Intrapersonal intelligence, 45–46 (figure)
Inventories
    informal reading, 51–52
    surveys and, 53–54, 55 (figure)
It Takes Two activity, 92

Jensen, Eric, 13, 22
Jigsaw groups, 148 (figure)
Journals, response, 155–156

Kaplan, H., 19
Kasser, T., 18
Kauchak, D. P., 6
Kim, Y., 18
King, R., 8, 9, 61, 74, 154
    on motivation, 13
    on reading comprehension, 125
    on syllables, 122
    on vocabulary, 81, 88, 89
Know Cans activity, 96
Knowledge base grouping design, 148 (figure)
Kraemer, J., 177
Kyle, D. W., 177

Language experience model, 67–69
Learning
    attention, challenge, excitement, and humor in, 21–22
    auditory, 37–38
    choices in, 22–23, 35–36, 79, 80 (figure)
    community teams, 149 (figure)
    constructivist, 6–7
    data-driven decisions regarding, 5–6
    emotional barriers to, 34–35
    flexible grouping for, 5
    flow, 20–21
    inclusion and, 6
    Individual Learning Plans (ILPs) and, 5, 57 (figure)
    interventions, 5
    memory and, 7
    new words, 84–86
    opportunities in errors, 16
    preferences, 42, 44
    schema theories of, 6
    strategy ownership and, 7
    styles, 47, 48 (figure)
    team spirit for, 16
    verbal linguistic intelligence and, 6
    zones, 63, 74–77
    See also Reading
Leppien, J. H., 62
Letter sound recognition, 103–104, 110–118
Levine, M., 56
Lip-reading, 38
Literal comprehension, 128
Literary circles, 149 (figure)
Logical/mathematical intelligence, 45–46 (figure)
Lower grades, language experiences in, 68

Magnetic resonance imaging (MRI), 20
Malapropisms, 155

Marzano, R., 101, 135
Match Game activity, 90–91
McCarthy, B., 48
McCarthy, D., 48
McIntyre, E., 177
McTighe, Jay, 167
Meanings, multiple, 105–106
Meet and Greet! assessment tool, 83
Meister, C., 147
Memory, 7
Mental pictures, 138
Menus and agendas, 72–74, 75 (figure)
Metaphors, 150
Miscues, overcoming, 102–105
Misfit nonsense, 155
Motivation, 18–19, 20 (figure), 30–31
Multiple intelligences, 44, 45–46 (figure)
Multiple Madness activity, 94
Multiple meanings, 105–106
Music, 154
Musical/rhythmic intelligence, 45–46 (figure)
Mystery Word assessment tool, 83–84
My Talking Brain activity, 158–159

National Reading Panel, 128
Naturalist intelligence, 45–46 (figure)
Negative attitudes, 19, 34
Nervous students, 34, 37
Nonreading students, 29–31
Note-taking, 135–136

Oczkus, L., 128
Omissions, letter, 104
Opinions, forming, 151
Oral reading checks, 160–161
Overcoming miscues, 102–105
Ownership, strategy, 7

Paper, types of, 76
Parallel Curriculum, 19
Paraphrasing, 150
Parent conferences, 179
Parr, J., 177
Partner reading, 140, 144–145, 149 (figure)
Peer pressure, 34
Peer-to-peer tutoring, 148 (figure), 151
Performance assessments. See Assessment tools
Perini, M. J., 131
Peterson, D., 168
Phonics skills, 32, 109
    accent rule and clues and, 122
    checklist, 123 (figure)
    consonants, 110–115
    phonograms, 116–117
    prefixes and, 119–120
    root words and, 118, 119 (figure)
    structural analysis and, 118–122, 123 (figure)
    suffixes and, 120, 121 (figure)
    syllables and, 121–122
    vowels, 115–118
Phonograms, 116–117
Physical classroom environment, 14–16

Piaget, Jean, 6
Pickering, D., 135
Planning
    for excellence, 180–181
    homework alternatives, 179–180
    instruction for English-language learners, 177–178
    interventions, 176 (figure)
    parent conferences, 179
    for reading of informational text, 170–172, 173
        (figure)
    schoolwide, 167–168
    special services for students with diagnosed reading
        problems, 176
    standards and, 174–175, 176 (figure)
    text checks and, 173–176
    tools checklist, 183–189
    to use activities effectively, 169–170
    to use reading strategies effectively, 168–170
    with variety, 168–169
Pollack, J., 135
Preassessments
    planning for comprehension, 130
    vocabulary words, 82–84
Prefixes, 119–120
Prereading, 129–136
Print-rich environments, 14
Problem-based model, 64
Problem-solving teams, 149 (figure)
Project-based models, 63–64
Project teams, 149 (figure)
Punctuation symbols, 32–33
Puppets, 157
Purposes for reading, 135

Questions
    effective, 159–160
    essential, 131–133

Random groups, 148 (figure)
Rapport, 17–18
Rates, reading, 129
Read-Aloud Handbook, The, 70
Read-alouds
    model, 70–71, 140
    student learning preference for, 37–38
    teacher, 143
Readiness for reading, developmental, 28
Reading
    achievements celebrations, 24–25
    alone, 143–144
    barriers to, 2–3, 5
    checks, oral, 160–161
    choice boards, 22–23, 85, 150 (figure)
    choral, 140, 142
    class, 141
    developmental readiness for, 28
    dyad, 145
    4MAT model and, 48, 49 (figure)
    guided, 65–67
    highlighting and color coding during, 138
    independent choice model, 65
    infused into content areas, 1, 4 (figure)

inventories, informal (IRIs), 51–52
journey, 10–11
keys to success in, 42, 43 (figure)
learning zones, 63, 74–77
motivation, 18–19, 20 (figure), 30–31
partner, 140, 144–145, 149 (figure)
passage view and, 136–140
places and spaces, 14–16
prereading and, 129–136
problems and solutions, 42, 43 (figure)
purposes for, 135
rates, 129
re-, 140
review after, 147–160
shared, 70
silent, 38–39
small-group, 146–147, 148 (figure)
stations, 63
staying on course with, 11
sticky mini tabbing during, 138–139
total group, 141–143
See also Learning
Readings
    volunteer, 141
Reasoning, 180
Recognition, letter sound, 103–104, 110–118
Recording Grid, 162, 163 (figure)
Reflection self-check, comprehension, 162
Rehearsing, 151
Renzulli, Joseph, 62
Repeating, 150
Repetitions, letter, 104–105
Rereading, 140
Research teams, 149 (figure)
Resilience, 181
Respect, 22
Response journals, 155–156
Responsibility, 181
Reversals, letter, 104
Review after reading, 147
Ribbon Wall, 99
Root words, 118, 119 (figure)
Rosenshine, B., 147
Roth, G., 19
Running record activity, 164, 165 (figure)

Safe and accepting atmosphere, 16–18
Same Game activity, 90
Scaffolding, 41
Scheidecker, D., 26
Schema, 138
    theories, 6
Scoring, showcase, 58
Searches for information, 150
Self-efficacy, 23–24
Senseless Sillies activity, 86–87
Shape Up strategy, 139–140
Share and Compare activity, 92–93
Shared reading model, 70
Sheldon, K. M., 18
Showcase scoring, 58
Shy students, 34

Sight vocabulary, 82
Sight words, 82
Silent reading, 38–39
Silver, H. F., 131
Similes, 150
Slavin, R. E., 144
Small-group reading, 146–147, 148 (figure)
Sort, fact, 152
Sounds, letter, 103–104, 110–118
Sousa, D., 20
Spotlight on Signals (SOS), 137
Sprenger, Marilee, 7
Stage It! activity, 142–143
Stage performances, 157
Standards, 174–175, 176 (figure)
Star clusters, 153–154
Station groups, 148 (figure)
Stations and centers, 63, 74–77
Sternberg, R. J., 47, 180
Stick Picks activity, 96
Sticky mini tabbing, 138–139
Stipek, D. J., 22
Stomp Romp activity, 96–97
Strategy ownership, 7
Strong, R. W., 131
Structural analysis, 118–122, 123 (figure)
Students
    assessing and diagnosing, 49–58
    barriers to reading for struggling, 2–3, 4
    beliefs survey, 54 (figure)
    celebrating reading achievements of, 24–25
    comfort level, 54 (figure)
    correcting behavior by, 36–37
    data-driven decisions regarding, 5–6
    developmental readiness for reading, 28
    diversity of, 27–28
    English-language learning, 177–178
    flexible grouping of, 5
    fluent, 40
    inclusion of, 6
    Individual Learning Plans (ILPs), 5, 57 (figure)
    insecure, 33–35
    interest surveys, 53 (figure), 55 (figure)
    interventions for, 5, 30, 31–33, 34–37, 38, 39, 40
    learning preferences of, 42, 44
    learning styles, 47, 48 (figure)
    mastery of vocabulary, 106–107
    multiple intelligences of, 6, 44, 45–46 (figure)
    nonreading, 29–31
    providing teaching opportunities for, 16–17
    read-aloud, 37–38
    reading journey and, 10–11
    role in planning for reading informational text, 172
    self-efficacy in, 23–24
    silent-reading, 38–39
    triarchic intelligences, 47
    turned-off, 35–36
    word-calling, 31–33
Styles, learning, 47, 48 (figure)
Subject terminology, 101–102
Substitutions, letter, 104
Successful readers, 40–42, 50 (figure)

Suffixes, 120, 121 (figure)
Summarizing, 152
Surveys and inventories, 53–54, 55 (figure)
Syllables, 121–122
Sylwester, Robert, 127

TAPS approach, 141–147, 169
Teachers
  guiding the reading journey, 10
  -made comprehension assessment, 52
  -made vocabulary checklists, 106–107
  -made vocabulary level assessment, 51–52
  reading aloud, 143
  role in building self-efficacy, 23–24
  role in comprehension instruction, 164–166
  role in guided reading, 65–67
  role in planning for reading informational text, 171–172
  role in providing choices, 23
  who become legends in learners' live, 26
Team spirit for learning, 16
Technology equipment, 77
Terminology, subject, 101–102
Text checks, 173–176
Text Talk strategy, 146–147
Think-Pair-Share-Reflect, 155
Think Tank strategy, 146
Tomlinson, Carol Ann, 19, 20 (figure), 62
Total group reading, 141–143
Trelease, Jim, 70
Triarchic intelligences, 47
Trio Masterpiece activity, 93
T-Toon activity, 94
Tuculescu, G., 131
Turned-off readers, 35–36
2, 4, 6, 8 graph, 130–131

Upper grades, language experiences in, 68–69

VanDer Wege, C., 168
Verbal/linguistic intelligence, 6, 45–46 (figure)
Visuals, vocabulary, 98–100
Visual/spatial intelligence, 45–46 (figure)
Vocabulary
  adjustable assignments, 86
  Analogy Action activity, 92
  Artful Antics activity, 91
  Beat! activity, 88–89
  Box It! activity, 87, 88 (figure)
  Cartoon Capers activity, 94
  checklists, 106–107
  Color My World activity, 82
  Compound Word Wizard activity, 91
  context clues, 100–101
  Crisscross Challenge activity, 93–94
  Curiosity Collection Corner activity, 97

Evening Learning Opportunity (ELO) activity, 89–90
  Five Up activity, 95–96
  four-block model and, 72 (figure)
  guided reading and, 66
  identifying and selecting, 81–82
  It Takes Two activity, 92
  Know Cans activity, 96
  learning new, 84–86
  level assessment, 51–52
  Match Game activity, 90–91
  Meet and Greet! activity, 83
  Multiple Madness activity, 94
  multiple meanings in, 105–106
  Mystery Word activity, 83–84
  overcoming miscues with, 102–105
  preassessing, 82–84
  Same Game activity, 90
  Share and Compare activity, 92–93
  sight, 82
  Sketch activity, 97
  Stick Picks activity, 96
  Stomp Romp activity, 96–97
  student mastery of, 106–107
  subject terminology, 101–102
  Trio Masterpiece activity, 93
  T-Toon activity, 94
  twenty-five ways to teach, 86–97
  Vine, 99
  visuals, 98–100
  as vocabulary, 85
  word discovery, 85–86
  Word Game Trivia activity, 97
  Words in Motion activity, 88
  Words on Word activity, 95
Vocabulary Beat! activity, 88–89
Vocabulary Sketch activity, 97
Vocabulary Vine, 99
Volunteer readings, 141
Von Secker, C., 18
Vowels, 115–118

Wigfield, A., 18
Wiggins, Grant, 167
Wolk, Steven, 26
Word attack skills, 30
Word-calling, 31–33
Word Game Trivia activity, 97
Words. *See* Vocabulary
Words in Motion activity, 88
Words on Word activity, 95
Word Substitution Wall, 98–99
Wright, J., 174
Writing
  four-block model and, 72 (figure)
  implements, 76

CORWIN
A SAGE Company

The Corwin logo—a raven striding across an open book—represents the union of courage and learning. Corwin is committed to improving education for all learners by publishing books and other professional development resources for those serving the field of PreK–12 education. By providing practical, hands-on materials, Corwin continues to carry out the promise of its motto: **"Helping Educators Do Their Work Better."**